The Young Person's
Guide to the Internet

Where can I find the best websites on the internet?

The Young Person's Guide to the Internet is an easy-to-use internet reference book that brings the very best of the internet to young people, students, parents, schools and teachers. It contains over 1600 websites, meticulously researched and selected with educational and leisure-time needs in mind. Informative and entertaining, this handy guide will help you to unlock the vast potential of the World Wide Web, and shows how it can be used safely and effectively with young people of all ages.

The websites are listed and summarised, and sorted into 30 categories, including all British National Curriculum subjects. This essential guide provides:

- a wealth of resources to assist parents, schools and teachers with general studies, educational enquiries and as back-up for both study and recreation;
- the best sites covering media, art and music, online games, theatre, attractions, sport, travel and much more;
- special sections for parents and teachers;
- comprehensive website summaries.

Using this invalua 'one-stop' guide will help you save time, effort and money, and do away with hours of was ul internet surfing.

Kate Hawthorne is a lecturer in business studies and founder and director of her own Public Relations compa y, Hatricks Public Relations Ltd.

Daniela Sheppard is an experienced webmaster, web editor and internet researcher.

The Young Person's Guide to the Internet

The essential website reference book for young people, parents and teachers

*K*ate *H*awthorne
*D*aniela *S*heppard

Routledge
Taylor & Francis Group

LONDON AND NEW YORK

First published 2001 by Hawthorne and Davis

Second edition published 2005
by Routledge
2 Park Square, Milton Park, Abingdon,
Oxon OX14 4RN

Simultaneously published in the USA
and Canada
by Routledge
270 Madison Ave, New York, NY 10016

Routledge is an imprint of the Taylor & Francis Group

© 2001, 2005 Kate Hawthorne and
Daniela Sheppard

Typeset in Eurostile by Keystroke,
Jacaranda Lodge, Wolverhampton
Printed and bound in Great Britain by
TJ International Ltd, Padstow, Cornwall

The publisher and authors cannot be held
responsible for the contents of any of the
websites, their links or recommendations
in this book. It should be viewed as general
information and not by way of specific
recommendation or advice. The websites
are provided for the users' convenience
and reference and the contents have been
drawn from a wide range of sources. The
authors and Routledge do not endorse or
accept responsibility for any views, advice,
opinions, omissions or recommendations
found in this book and shall not be held
liable for any claims, losses, injuries,
penalties, damages, costs or expenses
arising from its use and contents.

British Library Cataloguing in Publication Data
A catalogue record for this book is
available from the British Library

Library of Congress Cataloging in Publication Data
A catalog record for this book has been
requested

ISBN 0–415–34505–7 (pbk)

Contents

Preface	vii	Internet	89
Acknowledgements	ix	Internet Fun	96
		Languages	103
Categories		Lifestyle and Fashion	109
		Maths	116
Art	1	Media	121
Attractions	11	Museums	128
Careers and Students	20	Music	133
Crafts and Hobbies	27	Parents and Guardians	144
Dance	33	Politics	150
Drama and Theatre	38	Reference and Revision	156
Education and Teachers	43	Science	164
English	51	Social Studies	172
Environment	58	Special Needs	177
Film, Television and Radio	65	Sport and Activities	184
Geography	71	Travel	192
History	76	Younger Children	200
Information Technology	83		

Preface

The Young Person's Guide is aimed at children, students, parents and teachers. Part of our quest was to source the best websites available that covered subjects across the British National Curriculum, as well as providing topics that would be entertaining and useful for most age groups in primary and secondary education and beyond.

Both of us have teenage daughters, Lettie and Ana, who are studying for their GCSEs. The internet sometimes provides them with valuable help for their research and homework. However on many occasions, the more they looked for answers, the more difficult it became to find the right information, at the right level, without wasting time (and while avoiding unsuitable websites). We know that other students, parents, and teachers, frequently face this problem.

The internet is being used increasingly for both entertainment and as a key educational resource. But it can also be a minefield. Sites unsuitable for young people are all too easy to access – often accidentally. And with millions of websites it can be extremely difficult and time-consuming, even using search engines, to find those that are both relevant and appropriate. All the websites included in this book have been carefully chosen and researched with educational and recreational needs in mind. The book is designed to help unlock the vast educational and recreational potential of the Worldwide Web in a clear, safe and easy-to-use format, saving time, effort and money.

We have taken care to choose websites that should have longevity but in some cases you may find that the web address is no longer functional. Do try and look at other websites in that category for your information, as they will usually have a list of useful links which may provide the answers that you are looking for. It will be out there somewhere! Many new websites are coming on-line all the time. We have tried to include the most recent ones but please forgive any omissions and let us know of any exciting or excellent websites you may find so that we can include them in the future.

We hope you find the Young Person's Guide both useful and inspirational, and that it will become an invaluable reference resource. But above all, have fun!

For more information please visit www.youngpersonsguide.co.uk

Kate Hawthorne and Daniela Sheppard

Acknowledgements

Special thanks to:

Kate Hawthorne's mother Jennie Hawthorne – Author of over 20 books – 2 being published in 2005 her 89th year!

Richard Tucker for helping with Maths – www.tuckermaths.co.uk

Monica and Jesse Davis for their original belief and support

Alison Foyle from Routledge

Edited by Nick Sheppard

Minaz Ramzan – www.planetnewmedia.co.uk

Drama and Theatre photograph by Tristram Kenton, from a play directed by David Beaton

 **A**rt

In this category you can take a virtual tour of galleries and art museums and view some of the world's most famous works of art. Learn about architecture or the history of art, check the latest details on the National Curriculum and higher educational requirements, discover current trends in modern art or submit your own work for the world to see! Some artists' biographies are listed, but use the search facilities to find other famous artists' websites. **It is worth visiting the Museums category too as this has many related topics**.

About – Art History

About – Painting

AccessArt

AHDS Visual Arts

Architecture for All

Architecture Foundation

Art and Architecture

Art Crimes

Art Guide

Art History Resources

Art Museum Network

Art Republic

Art UK

Artchive

ArtCyclopedia

ArtLex

Arts Council England

ArtSource

ArtStudent Net

Artworks

Ashmolean Museum of Art and
   Archaeology

BBC Arts

Berger Foundation

British Arts Festivals Association

British Council – Arts

Cartoon Art Trust

Cartoon Factory

Click Click

Computers and the History of Art

Contemporary Art Society

Design and Artists Copyright Society

Design Council

Design Museum

DesignAddict

DeviantART

Grove Art Online

Institute of International Visual Arts

International Sculpture Centre

Metropolitan Museum of Art

Museum of Domestic Design and
  Architecture

Museum of Web Art

My Studios

The National Gallery

The National Portrait Gallery

New York Institute of Photography

Public Monuments and Sculpture
  Association

The Royal Academy of Arts

Royal British Society of Sculptors

Royal College of Art

Royal Institute of British Architects

Royal Photographic Society

Royal Society of British Artists

Society for All Artists

Society of Women Artists

Surrealism

The-artists

University of the Arts London

Web Gallery of Art

Worldwide Arts Resources

ZeWall – Online Painting

A2

Artists

Charles Rennie Mackintosh

Francis Bacon

Leonardo da Vinci

Matisse

Michelangelo

Pablo Picasso

Renoir

Salvador Dali

Vincent Van Gogh

About – Art History

www.arthistory.about.com

This website has detailed, comprehensive
articles and resources looking at the
history of art.

About – Painting

www.painting.about.com

About – Painting provides comprehensive,
well-maintained articles and resources
for anyone who wants to learn more
about painting. The website has
information on techniques, trends, famous
artists, links to good art websites and
much more.

AccessArt

www.accessart.org.uk

AccessArt provides fun, creative learning tools for pupils at all key stages and is a valuable resource bank for teachers. Users can access a wide variety of resources including online workshops, teachers' notes and learners' print-outs.

AHDS Visual Arts

www.vads.ahds.ac.uk

AHDS Visual Arts aims to provide and preserve collections of visual arts digital resources and to promote good practice for their creation and use.

Architecture For All

www.architectureforall.com

This ambitious project aims to bring awareness of architecture and the built environment to the widest possible audience by building a home to preserve and display the drawings and archive collections of the Royal Institute of British Architects.

Architecture Foundation

www.architecturefoundation.org.uk

The Architecture Foundation aims to inspire and cultivate new ideas in architecture and to foster a culture of collaboration and participation between the public, architects, the government, academics and business.

Art and Architecture

www.artandarchitecture.org.uk

A stylish website aimed at public libraries, schools and those interested in the links between art and architecture. The site displays drawings, paintings and photographs previously inaccessible to the public.

Art Crimes

www.graffiti.org

Art Crimes is dedicated to artists who express themselves through graffiti on the world's walls. This stylish site includes many photos and images and looks at graffiti around the world.

Art Guide

www.artguide.org

'The Art Lovers Guide to Britain and Ireland'. A very helpful and comprehensive guide with alphabetical listings of over 1,900 artists, detailing their works and where they can be seen together with extensive listings of art museums and exhibitions.

Art History Resources

http://witcombe.sbc.edu/ARTHLinks.html

A huge directory of online art history resources neatly arranged both chronologically and geographically. The website also includes a directory of museums and galleries around the world.

Art Museum Network

www.amn.org

A selection of some of the world's largest art museums collaborate on this website to provide information about their collections, exhibitions and news. View work from The Hermitage, Metropolitan Museum of Art (MOMA), The Tate Gallery, *et al*. Link to www.AMICO.org, the Art Museum Image Consortium with an illustrated search engine of 100,000 works of art and a digital library educational resource.

A3

Art Republic

www.artrepublic.co.uk

In addition to supplying posters and prints, Art Republic has comprehensive listings of exhibitions at galleries and public art museums around the world.

Art UK

www.artuk.co.uk

A stylish website with over 450 pages showing more than 1,400 images from artists around the world. Plus online chat, tutorials and multimedia projects.

Artchive

www.artchive.com

Artchive provides biographical information on individual artists, images, links to art books available on the net and links to other resources. The website also includes art CD-Rom reviews, theory and criticism plus virtual galleries.

Artcyclopedia

www.artcyclopedia.com

A search engine that aims to become the 'definitive and most effective guide to museum-quality fine art on the internet'. It only lists sites where an artist's work can be viewed online.

ArtLex

www.artlex.com

An art dictionary for artists, collectors, students and educators with more than 3,600 terms defined.

Arts Council England

www.arts.org.uk

The Arts Council England is the national development agency for the arts in England. It invests public funds, including from the National Lottery. Its vision is to promote the arts at the heart of national life, reflecting England's diverse cultural identity.

ArtSource

www.ilpi.com/artsource

Quality rather than quantity is the motto for this US portal site that has links to some of the best art resources available on the internet, including electronic exhibitions from the visual arts at the Australian National University and resources for classics and art history teachers from the Beazley Archive at the University of Oxford.

Art Student net

www.art-student.net

This website contains resources and material required for Key Stage 3, GCSE, AS and A level for UK schools and is approved by Curriculum Online and the NGfl. This site is an extensive database of art and design resources accessed via subscription, and takes the visitor to contemporary art resources as well as studio practice.

Artworks

www.art-works.org.uk

The Artworks programme supports visual arts education in the UK. Through the Artworks Award Scheme, Children's Arts Day and its research projects. Artworks aims to increase opportunities for young people to be inspired and challenged through art and design.

The Ashmolean Museum of Art and Archaeology

www.ashmol.ox.ac.uk

The Ashmolean Museum in Oxford is one of the oldest public museums in the world and houses collections of brass rubbings, cast galleries, ceramics, coins, medals, paintings, prints, sculpture, metalwork, glass, instruments and jewellery, as well as drawings by Michelangelo and Raphael. There are collections from the palaeolithic to Victorian and from Egypt, the Middle East, Europe and Britain.

BBC Arts

www.bbc.co.uk/arts

The BBC's informative and well-designed arts site includes news, features, online exhibitions and more.

Berger Foundation

www.bergerfoundation.ch

This is a comprehensive archive of over 100,000 slides belonging to the Jacques-Edouard Berger Foundation. It features art from all of the world's main civilisations, both Eastern and Western.

British Arts Festivals Association

www.artsfestivals.co.uk

The BAFA website includes a calendar, directory and map detailing arts festivals across the UK.

British Council – Arts

www.britishcouncil.org/arts

Promoting British arts abroad, the British Council provides a wealth of articles, features and news about the best of British arts and artists.

Cartoon Art Trust

www.cartooncentre.com

The Cartoon Art Trust is dedicated to preserving and promoting the best of British cartoon art and caricature. It also aims to establish a museum of cartoon art.

Cartoon Factory

www.cartoon-factory.com

Cartoon Factory has cool information about the basics of animation art plus a big animation art gallery and an online shop.

Click Click

www.clickclick.com

A US photography portal site with links to an extensive list of sites covering every aspect of photography.

Computers and the History of Art

www.chart.ac.uk

CHArt is a society open to all who have an interest in the application of computers to the study of art and design. It also houses the Worldwide Web Virtual Library for History of Art.

Contemporary Art Society

www.contempart.org.uk

The CAS is a registered charity which promotes the collecting of contemporary art through gifts to public museums and advice and guidance to companies and individuals. It has presented over 5,000 works of contemporary art to museums throughout the UK since 1910.

Design and Artists Copyright Society

www.dacs.org.uk

The society promotes and protects the copyright for the visual work created by artists based in the UK and worldwide.

The Design Council

www.design-council.org.uk

The Design Council helps businesses, education, the government and public services to understand the importance of design as a contributor to improved prosperity and well-being. Their attractive website is full of inspiration for those interested in design issues.

Design Museum

www.designmuseum.org

Devoted to modern design, fashion and architecture, this museum in London is the largest provider of design education resources in the UK. It also manages the Designer of the Year award.

DesignAddict

www.designaddict.com

An ample design database packed with useful information about modern, post-modern and contemporary design. It is useful for collectors, students and the curious.

DeviantART

www.deviantart.com

DeviantART is dedicated to alternative art. Some good, some bad, some cool . . . some not. It has thousands of art images from traditional to digital works to cellphone art. The website provides excellent inspiration for your art projects and you can also submit your own work or comment on art already posted.

Grove Art Online

www.groveart.com

Grove Art Online is a subscription-based resource covering every aspect of visual art from pre-history to the present day, including over 45,000 articles, over 130,000 art images and a huge search facility.

Institute of International Visual Arts

www.iniva.org

A website dedicated to bringing the work of artists from culturally-diverse backgrounds to the attention of the public through exhibitions, publications, multimedia, education and research projects.

International Sculpture Centre

www.sculpture.org

The ISC seeks to expand public understanding and appreciation of sculpture. You can see images of contemporary sculpture with artists' statements and biographies. There is also a sculpture magazine, discussion groups and technical resources.

Metropolitan Museum of Art

www.metmuseum.org

The Metropolitan Museum of Art is one of the finest and largest art museums in the world with more than 2 million works of art covering 5,000 years of world culture and history. It has an impressive online presence with extensive resources.

Museum of Domestic Design and Architecture

www.moda.mdx.ac.uk

MoDA holds one of the world's most comprehensive collections of decorative arts for the home, covering the nineteenth and twentieth centuries. You can see parts of each collection online. A valuable resource for anyone interested in the history of design for the home.

Museum of Web Art

www.mowa.org

This stylish virtual museum promotes the culture of the worldwide web through exhibitions of the smart art of the internet, with galleries covering 'things that move, things that work, things that are constant and things that change'. Plus the website has a special kids wing.

My Studios

www.mystudios.com

An attractive site with great resources (many downloadable) for students and art enthusiasts. Each well presented section includes extensive texts, images and online exhibits covering a wide variety of art topics.

The National Gallery

www.nationalgallery.org.uk

The National Gallery houses one of the greatest collections of European paintings in the world.

The National Portrait Gallery

www.npg.org.uk

Founded in 1856 to collect the likenesses of famous British men and women, the National Portrait Gallery now houses the most comprehensive collection of its kind in the world. The website offers a catalogue of 10,000 portraits from collections of drawings, prints, paintings, sculpture and photography.

New York Institute of Photography

www.nyip.com

This prestigious institution has a valuable web presence and provides extensive resources for all people interested in photography. Apart from providing a variety of home study photography courses, the site offers a monthly magazine packed with tips and inspirational features.

Public Monuments and Sculpture Association

www.pmsa.org.uk

Established in 1991, the PMSA aims to heighten public awareness of the UK's monumental heritage and campaigns for the preservation, protection and restoration of public monuments and sculptures.

The Royal Academy of Arts

www.royalacademy.org.uk/ collection

The Royal Academy, founded in 1768 to promote and inspire new generations of British artists is now making its collection accessible online. The collection comprises many works of art given by artists themselves and includes self-portraits by Reynolds and Gainsborough.

Royal British Society of Sculptors

www.rbs.org.uk

The RBS is a membership society for professional sculptors and was founded in 1904. It is a registered charity which exists to promote and advance the art of sculpture.

Royal College of Art

www.rca.ac.uk

The only wholly postgraduate university of art and design in the world. The website allows students from around the world the opportunity to exhibit their work on graduation.

Royal Institute of British Architects

www.riba.org

RIBA are one of the most influential architectural institutions in the world. RIBA's mission is to advance architecture and promote excellence in the profession.

Royal Photographic Society

www.rps.org

The work of the RPS which promotes the art and science of photography. Their website includes the latest photography news and details of exhibitions and you can also discuss photography or view the work of RPS members.

Royal Society of British Artists

www.the-rba.org.uk

The RBA is an institution for the aid and promotion of the Arts and was formed in 1823. The RBA welcomes submissions of work from young artists for possible inclusion in their annual exhibition.

Society for All Artists

www.saa.co.uk

The SAA's aim is to inform, encourage and inspire all artists. It has over 28,000 members in 62 countries while over 600 art clubs and societies are affiliated to the SAA. It offers a range of services and advice to artists and has an excellent gallery featuring the best of members' artwork.

Society of Women Artists

www.society-women-artists. org.uk

Established to give serious women artists an opportunity to exhibit, the Society of Women Artists aims to promote art by women and has some of the world's finest contemporary women artists as its elected members.

Surrealism

www.surrealism.co.uk

An online community space for artists and audiences interested in contemporary art, featuring the work of over 300 contemporary artists.

The-artists

www.the-artists.org

An attractive and easy to use database of twentieth century and contemporary visual artists, listed alphabetically, by movement and by discipline. It is a helpful resource for students.

University of the Arts London

www.arts.ac.uk

Consisting of 5 internationally renowned colleges, the University of the Arts London is at the forefront of learning

A 8

and creativity and offers a range of academic programmes.

Web Gallery of Art

www.wga.hu

A virtual museum and database with over 11,000 reproductions of European painting and sculpture covering the Gothic, Renaissance and Baroque periods (1150–1800).

Worldwide Arts Resources

www.wwar.com

This website provides extensive resources including contemporary artists and masters, museums, galleries, art history and education. Or you can browse online through over 200,000 works by more than 22,000 masters.

ZeWall – Online Painting

www.zewall.com

An online art tool allowing you to create graffiti art on a virtual wall. Submit your own work or vote for other people's artistry.

Artists

Charles Rennie Mackintosh

www.charlesrenniemac.co.uk

A website devoted to Charles Rennie Mackintosh.

Francis Bacon

www.francis-bacon.cx

This website is devoted to Francis Bacon.

Leonardo da Vinci

www.kausal.com/leonardo

This website is devoted to Leonardo da Vinci.

Matisse

www.musee-matisse-nice.org

A website devoted to Matisse.

Michelangelo

www.michelangelo.com/buonarroti. html

A website devoted to Michelangelo.

Pablo Picasso

www.picasso.fr

www.picassoforthemaninthestreet. org

A website devoted to Picasso.

Renoir

www.renoir.org.yu

A website devoted to Renoir.

Salvador Dali

www.salvadordalimuseum.org

A website devoted to Dali.

Vincent Van Gogh

www.vangoghgallery.com

Website devoted to Van Gogh.

ATTRACTIONS

This section covers some of the UK's best known and most interesting attractions, covering all age groups as well as school visits. Many of the sites contain interesting historical and educational information in addition to tourist directories with links to exciting and unusual places to explore. **Visit the Museums, Sport and Activities, Crafts and Hobbies, Travel and the Art categories for further inspiration.**

Alnwick Castle

Alton Towers

Blackpool Pleasure Beach

Bristol Zoo Gardens

Cadbury World

Chessington World of Adventures

Clink Prison

Cotswold Water Park

The Deep

Diggerland

Dinosaur Adventure Park

Drayton Manor Theme Park

Eden Project

Edinburgh Festivals

Edinburgh Zoo

eFestivals

English Heritage

Festivals.com

Gardens Guide

Golden Hinde

Good Zoo Guide Online

Great British Gardens

Historic Royal Palaces

HMS Belfast

Howletts Wild Animal Park

Leeds Castle

Legoland

London Aquarium

London Eye

London Town

London Zoo

Longleat

Look Out Discovery Centre

Lord's – The Home of Cricket

ATTRACTIONS

Madame Tussauds

Marwell Zoological Park

Mary Rose

Monkey World Ape Rescue Centre

National Gardens Scheme

National Motor Museum

National Trust

Newquay Zoo

Oakwood

Paignton Zoo Environmental Park

Pleasureland

Portsmouth Historic Dockyard

Royal Botanic Gardens, Kew

Royal Horticultural Society

Royal Pavilion

Safari Park

Sherwood Forest Farm Park

Snowdon Mountain Railway

Somerset House

St Paul's Cathedral

Tales of Robin Hood

Thorpe Park

Tourist Attractions and Travel Information

Tower Bridge Exhibition

UK Heritage Railways

Warwick Castle

Waterscape

Westminster Abbey

Westminster Cathedral

Whipsnade Wild Animal Park

Woburn Safari Park

ZooWatch

Alnwick Castle

www.alnwickcastle.com

An attractive website about Alnwick Castle, a stunning and dramatic medieval castle in Northumberland.

Alton Towers

www.altontowers.com

Featuring a superb waterpark, amazing rides of all descriptions, a luxurious Spa and Ice Shows, the Alton Towers website will help you plan your ultimate day out at one of the best known theme parks in the UK.

Blackpool Pleasure Beach

www.blackpoolpleasurebeach.co.uk

With over 145 rides and attractions, Blackpool Pleasure Beach is the UK's top free tourist attraction and welcomes over seven million visitors annually.

Bristol Zoo Gardens

www.bristolzoo.org.uk

Bristol Zoo Gardens was awarded the prestigious title of Zoo of the Year by the Good Britain Guide 2004. It was highlighted as a 'must see' destination for 2004 with descriptions such as 'excellent value, with lots to see'. Their website will help you plan your visit.

Cadbury World

www.cadburyworld.co.uk

At the world-famous Cadbury World in Bourneville, Birmingham you can discover the history and magic of chocolate making. You can find out more from their website.

Chessington World of Adventures

www.chessington.com

Find out from this about the new adventures and rides available this year and buy your tickets online. School talks can also be arranged as part of a memorable educational day out at Chessington in Surrey.

Clink Prison

www.clink.co.uk

A fascinating museum at a prison in the heart of London from where the phrase "in the clink" originates. The museum's website offers a virtual visit inside the prison, where you can learn what it was like to be locked up in Tudor times.

Cotswold Water Park

www.waterpark.org

A guide to the 132 man-made lakes in the Cotswold Water Park, the largest such complex in the UK.

The Deep

www.thedeep.co.uk

Europe's deepest fish tank is in Hull's city centre. The Deep is an environmental charity dedicated to understanding and protecting the world's oceans. Their website is an excellent educational tool and includes tailored lesson plans.

Diggerland

www.diggerland.com

This digger hire firm had to deal with so many questions from inquisitive children that it decided to open its own theme park. Diggerland is where youngsters (and their parents) can drive giant dump trucks, JCBs and 10-ton diggers, all under strict supervision. The parks are in Kent, Devon and Durham.

Dinosaur Adventure Park

www.dinosaurpark.co.uk

Set in a beautiful woodland in Norfolk, Dinosaur Adventure Park offers visitors the opportunity to come face to face with lifesize dinosaurs, meet creatures from way back in time, explore the maze, make friends with the animals and much more.

Drayton Manor Theme Park

www.draytonmanor.co.uk

A stunning website about one of the UK's most popular theme parks which is based in Staffordshire. Find out from the website about new rides and attractions.

Eden Project

www.edenproject.com

The Eden Project is one of the main attractions of Cornwall. Its mission is to 'promote the understanding and responsible management of the vital relationship between plants, people and resources leading to a sustainable future for all'. It is a must for a family day out.

Edinburgh Festivals

www.edinburghfestivals.co.uk

The official website with full listings of all Edinburgh Festivals.

A 13

Edinburgh Zoo

www.edinburghzoo.org.uk

Described as Scotland's most exciting wildlife attraction, Edinburgh Zoo was opened in 1913 and is recognised as one of the world's leading zoos. You can find out more from their website.

eFestivals

www.efestivals.co.uk

A guide to outdoor music festivals in the UK with news, information, reviews, photos and tickets.

English Heritage

www.english-heritage.org.uk

English Heritage's mission is to make sure that England's historic environment is properly maintained. Their detailed and attractive website provides information about the projects they manage and guidance about historic places to visit.

Festivals.com

www.festivals.com

A colourful site that claims to be the largest source on the internet for information about festivals, fairs and community events around the world. There are over 40,000 events listed on the website.

Gardens Guide

www.gardenvisit.com

A directory of gardens around the world that are open to visitors. There are over 800 gardens listed here for the UK.

Golden Hinde

www.goldenhinde.co.uk

An accurate reconstruction of Sir Francis Drake's tudor galleon, berthed on the Thames, the Golden Hinde is a living history museum and runs full-time educational programmes for schools and families. Visit the website to find out how you can spend a night aboard, learning about life at sea in the 16th century.

Good Zoo Guide Online

www.goodzoos.com

A comprehensive guide to zoos, wildlife parks and animal collections around the world. The website gives you the chance to contribute your own reviews.

Great British Gardens

www.greatbritishgardens.co.uk

A beautiful guide to gardens to visit around the UK and places to stay nearby.

Historic Royal Palaces

www.hrp.org.uk

All you need to know about visiting five magnificent buildings around London – the Tower of London, Kensington Palace, Hampton Court Palace, the Banqueting House and Kew Palace. These are some of the most visited attractions in the UK.

HMS Belfast

http://hmsbelfast.iwm.org.uk

The huge cruiser HMS Belfast, which was launched in 1938 and served throughout the Second World War, has been moored on the Thames since 1971 and is a magnificent reminder of Britain's rich naval heritage.

A 14

Howletts Wild Animal Park

www.howletts.net

Described by the BBC as one of the best wild animal parks in the world, Howletts is near Canterbury in Kent, and has over 70 acres of ancient parkland. It is very different from traditional zoos and parks in that the animals roam freely in as near to natural enclosures as possible. Six live webcams provide an opportunity to glimpse the animals live.

Leeds Castle

www.leeds-castle.com

Considered to be one of the most beautiful castles in the world, Leeds Castle in Kent was first mentioned in the Doomsday Book and is one of the most romantic and historic buildings in the UK.

Legoland

www.legoland.co.uk

The Legoland website has full details of the park's rides, attractions and events plus all the information you need to plan your visit to the 'Land of Creativity' at Windsor.

London Aquarium

www.londonaquarium.co.uk

The practical information you need about visiting the London Aquarium, with information about their attractions – from the coral reefs and Indian Ocean to the depths of the Pacific and Atlantic Oceans.

London Eye

www.ba-londoneye.com

Facts and figures about the big wheel, plus loads of views and pictures. Is it a great addition to London's horizon or an out-of-place eyesore? Whatever your

opinion, it is one of the best places to get views across London.

London Town

www.londontown.com

An excellent, comprehensive online guide to London that is packed full of advice about what to see and do in London, where to stay and how to get about.

London Zoo

www.londonzoo.co.uk

One of the world's most famous zoos, London Zoo houses 5,000 animals from 650 species – 112 of which are classified as threatened. Their clear website will help you to plan your visit.

Longleat

www.longleat.co.uk

Voted 'UK Family Attraction of the Year' in 2002, Longleat in Wiltshire offers a 'wonderland of attraction' for visitors of all ages. The first safari park outside Africa, in the grounds of the first stately home to open its doors to the public, Longleat remains one of the UK's most popular attractions.

Look Out Discovery Centre

www.bracknell-forest.gov.uk/lookout

The Look Out Discovery Centre is a hands-on science and nature exhibition which provides hours of educational fun for children.

Lord's – The Home of Cricket

www.mcc.org.uk

A must visit for all cricket fans. The site gives a brief history of Marylebone Cricket

A 15

Club and also the most up-to-date version of the Laws of Cricket, for use in all competitions. On the website you can also check the events at Lord's or look up the guided ground tours available.

Madame Tussauds

www.madame-tussauds.co.uk

A sparkling website from the home of one of London's most visited attractions. Don't forget if you book online you benefit from guaranteed timed entry, so no queuing. Prime Ministers, footballers and pop stars, famous people from around the world can be seen here in lifesize waxwork sculptures.

Marwell Zoological Park

www.marwell.org.uk

Marwell Zoological Park in Hampshire has many species of animals, including many that are endangered. Their aim is to help people increase their knowledge of the natural world and to raise awareness of conservation issues.

Mary Rose

www.maryrose.org

The fascinating story of the Mary Rose, the only 16th century warship on display anywhere in the world. Sunk in 1545 during a sea battle, the Mary Rose was raised in 1982 and it is now on display at Portsmouth.

Monkey World Ape Rescue Centre

www.monkeyworld.org

Set in 65 acres of Dorset woodland, Monkey World is a sanctuary for over 150 primates from 15 different species.

National Gardens Scheme

www.ngs.org.uk

This website has details of over 2,000 fine gardens open to the public to raise money for charities.

National Motor Museum

www.beaulieu.co.uk

The National Motor Museum at Beaulieu in Hampshire is world renowned. Their website provides a colourful introduction and if you are a car enthusiast this is one place you must visit.

National Trust

www.nationaltrust.org.uk

The National Trust, a registered charity, was founded in 1895 'to act as a guardian for the nation in the acquisition and protection of threatened coastline, countryside and buildings'. At present the Trust cares for over 248,000 hectares of countryside, almost 600 miles of coastline and more than 200 buildings and gardens in England, Wales and Northern Ireland. Most of the gardens are open to visitors with their upkeep largely managed by volunteers. Wherever you live in the UK you will not be far from several National Trust properties.

Newquay Zoo

www.newquayzoo.co.uk

Newquay Zoo has become one of the UK's top zoos and has won 11 major awards since 1996. It specialises in breeding many endangered species and is at the forefront of conservation, education and entertainment.

Oakwood

www.oakwood-leisure.com

The website of the biggest theme park in Wales. You can view the rides and attractions before you visit.

Paignton Zoo Environmental Park

www.paigntonzoo.org.uk

Paignton Zoo is home to some of the world's most endangered animals and plants. Their bright and attractive website tells you everything you need to know about visiting the zoo and has information about its habitats and animals. The atmospheric Rainforest Room and Green Room are each full of exciting exhibits for children to see, touch and feel.

Pleasureland

www.pleasureland.uk.com

Opened in 1920 in Southport, Pleasureland continues to entertain thousands of visitors every day. The park continues to grow and improve with new attractions every year.

Portsmouth Historic Dockyard

www.historicdockyard.co.uk

Hundreds of years of British naval history can be experienced here on this website where you can learn how HMS Victory is being restored to her original condition, explore the Royal Naval Museum or take a tour around Portsmouth Harbour in a modern boat.

Royal Botanic Gardens, Kew

www.kew.org.uk

This site takes visitors on a guided tour of the Gardens' ten climatic zones and accesses botanical information about the plants inside. The site's technology allows the colourful world of plants to come alive.

Royal Horticultural Society

www.rhs.org.uk

The RHS, founded in 1804, is one of the world's leading horticultural organisations and the UK's leading gardening charity. The Society organises many events, including the world famous Chelsea Flower Show. This site gives plenty of information about RHS activities including its Schools' Membership Scheme and INSET, an in-service training programme for teachers.

Royal Pavilion

www.royalpavilion.org.uk

The Royal Pavilion in Brighton has a unique style that 'mixes Asian exoticism with British eccentricity'. Their visually stunning website will inspire you to visit this beautiful building.

Safari Park

www.safaripark.co.uk

A useful directory with details of wildlife and safari parks around the UK. Their impressive site also has information about animal behaviour, endangered species, competitions, downloads and a chat forum.

Sherwood Forest Farm Park

www.sherwoodforestfarmpark. co.uk

Sherwood Forest Farm Park is a centre approved by the Rare Breeds Survival Trust for the breeding of rare and protected farm animals. The park contains over 40 such breeds as well as more unusual animals such as fallow deer, exotic birds, wildfowl, wallabies and water buffalo.

Snowdon Mountain Railway

www.snowdonrailway.co.uk

Built in 1896, the Snowdon Mountain Railway is still regarded as a major engineering feat and has recently been voted the Wales Family Attraction of the Year.

Somerset House

www.somerset-house.org.uk

This magnificent 18th century building in central London houses the Courtauld Institute for Art, Gilbert Collection and Hermitage Rooms. It is also the venue for open-air concerts. Visit their website to find out what's on.

St Paul's Cathedral

www.stpauls.co.uk

Following the Great Fire of London in 1666, which severely damaged the old cathedral, Sir Christopher Wren was commissioned by Charles II to build a new Cathedral. On this website you can take a virtual tour of Wren's magnificent masterpiece and learn its history and place in the City of London.

Tales of Robin Hood

www.robinhood.uk.com

You can experience medieval life, legend and adventure at The Tales of Robin Hood, Nottingham's most popular tourist attraction.

Thorpe Park

www.thorpepark.co.uk

A theme park specialising in dare-devil rides with a 'fear-factor' index to help you make your choice. Thorpe Park is situated in Surrey about 20 miles from Central London.

Tourist Attractions and Travel Information

www.entsweb.co.uk/tourist

This website provides tourist information on attractions including castles, theme parks, museums, zoos and more.

Tower Bridge Exhibition

www.towerbridge.org.uk

One of the most recognisable bridges in the world, Tower Bridge has straddled the River Thames since 1894. The Tower Bridge Exhibition website gives some history and tells you about visiting this famous London landmark.

UK Heritage Railways

www.ukhrail.uel.ac.uk

A guide to the heritage railway scene in the UK and Ireland, including details of special events, trains and operating days for steam railways.

Warwick Castle

www.warwick-castle.co.uk

Warwick Castle – Britain's greatest medieval experience – is one of the UK's most popular attractions. Their evocative website gives a great taste of what is on offer.

Waterscape

www.waterscape.com

A guide to the UK's waterways, rural and urban. It also offers information about walks, cycle trips, days out and holidays taking in canals and rivers.

Westminster Abbey

www.westminster-abbey.org

One of London's most famous landmarks, Westminster Abbey is an architectural masterpiece from the 13th to 16th centuries and provides a unique pageant of British history. The Abbey's website provides a wealth of information and you can take an online tour.

Westminster Cathedral

www.westminstercathedral.org.uk

Visit this website to get a taste of the beautiful Westminster Cathedral, one of London's greatest secrets. The Byzantine style facade of balconies, towers and domes set this building apart from other London landmarks and the more familiar Gothic style of most British cathedrals.

Whipsnade Wild Animal Park

www.whipsnade.co.uk

Whipsnade, in Bedfordshire, covers 600 acres of parkland and has over 3,000 animals from 150 different species. They organise educational and school visits and you can adopt an animal. Adopting an animal is a unique and unusual gift and provides a crucial lifeline to Whipsnade's vital conservation work in over 30 countries.

Woburn Safari Park

www.woburnsafari.co.uk

Drive through Woburn Safari Park in Bedfordshire and take a close-up view of the animals. The website has all the information you need about visiting the park, including planning visits for teachers at primary and secondary schools.

ZooWatch

www.zoowatch.freeserve.co.uk

A UK directory site with links to zoos, safari parks and wildlife parks in the UK and Ireland.

A19

Careers and Students

This category focuses on resources for students, whether they are seeking variety in their gap year or looking for that all-important first job. There is lots of advice on issues such as finance, accommodation and health, plus further and higher education opportunities. A useful gap directory contains everything from opportunities for voluntary work abroad to travel arrangements and expeditions. Those about to start their careers will find lots of helpful information here. **See also Fashion and Lifestyle and Travel categories.**

Accommodation for Students

AdviceOnline

Aimhigher

Anywork Anywhere

AuPairs JobMatch

Big Choice

Camp America

Careers Portal

Council on International Educational
   Exchange

EduFind

Expedition Advisory Centre

Fast Tomato

Findagap

Gap Activity Projects

Gap Year

Graduate Careers Centre

Graduate Prospects

Higher Education and Research
   Opportunities

Hotrecruit

Inland Revenue

i-uk – education

Jobsearch

Lazy Student

Learning and Skills Council

National Union of Students

Open University

PAYAway

Prospects Street

Student

Student Loan Company

Student Money

Student Radio Association

StudentUK

StudentZone

Study UK

Support4Learning

Teacher Training Agency

TheSite

The Student Room

UKCourseFinder

Universities and Colleges Admissions
    Service

Woman Student Online

World-Wide Opportunities on Organic
    Farms (WWOOF)

Year Out Group

YMCA

Young Enterprise

Your Creative Future

Accommodation for Students

www.accommodation-for-students.com

A website providing help for students (and their parents) who are hunting for suitable accommodation in London.

AdviceOnline

www.adviceonline.co.uk

An easy to use site offering independent financial advice.

Aimhigher

www.aimhigher.ac.uk

An interesting, lively and helpful site that inspires young people to go into Higher Education (HE) and shows how HE can improve career prospects and help you find your dream job. Useful information is given on student life and finances.

Anywork Anywhere

www.anyworkanywhere.com

Anywork Anywhere advertises jobs for young people in the UK and worldwide.

Plus it offers advice on visas and accommodation. This is a good website for students taking a gap year or who want to earn some money during the summer holidays.

AuPairs JobMatch

www.aupairs.co.uk

A multilingual international matching service (not agency) for families seeking au pairs and for au pairs looking for work. The service is available only to registered members.

Big Choice

www.thebigchoice.com

Hundreds of job opportunities are listed here for graduates plus a comprehensive graduate recruitment careers guide which includes advice on writing a CV and tips about application forms. It is a good place to start your quest for your perfect career.

C 21

C 22

Camp America

www.campamerica.co.uk

Cam America helps you to explore the opportunity of taking a summer job working with children in the US.

Careers Portal

www.careers-portal.co.uk

A portal site that is part of the National Grid for Learning offering advice about choosing the right university, taking a gap year, finding a job and managing a career.

Council on International Educational Exchange

www.ciee.org.uk

Work, study, travel, learn and teach abroad through CIEE's international cultural exchange programmes.

EduFind

www.edufind.com

Students and professionals can find a wide range of international education resources at EduFind – schools offering courses to international students, English language courses, teaching English as a foreign language, information on business schools, colleges, universities and vocational schools are all here.

Expedition Advisory Centre

www.rgs.org/eac

A unit of the Royal Geographical Society, the EAC provides information, training and advice to anyone embarking on a scientific or adventurous expedition overseas.

Fast Tomato

www.fasttomato.com

An interesting website offering help on making those all-important decisions about education and careers. You can complete the online questionnaires and let Fast Tomato generate suggestions covering school subjects, further and higher education courses, career areas and more.

Findagap

www.findagap.com

The online gap directory compiled by those that have been there and done that!

Gap Activity Projects

www.gap.org.uk

Gap Activity Projects is a not-for-profit charity arranging more than 1,500 placements in 34 countries for UK volunteers.

Gap Year

www.gapyear.com

The online home of Gapyear magazine. The website contains oodles of advice about how to make the most of a gap year, with tips and experiences from former gap year students. The website also has useful information on money, insurance, health and visas.

Graduate Careers Centre

www.hobsons.co.uk

A career orientated site advertising not only jobs for graduates but also providing information about career opportunities for a variety of industries along with further education, training and development opportunities worldwide.

Graduate Prospects

www.prospects.ac.uk

Prospects is the UK's official graduate career website. It covers jobs, career advice plus it has a section with country information for graduates interested in working abroad.

Higher Education and Research Opportunities

www.hero.ac.uk

This website provides guidance, information, advice and essential contacts for all aspects of higher education and research opportunities in the UK. The latest news from the UK educational world is also available here along with reports and reviews.

Hotrecruit

www.hotrecruit.co.uk

Hotrecruit lists up-to-date vacancies which can be searched by industry, region, hours or keywords defining the job category. Job information is provided for such diverse activities as diving in Greece, casino croupiers or film stunt work. It has information about gap year and summer jobs too.

Inland Revenue

www.inlandrevenue.gov.uk

This website explains how taxes are collected, and why. It also provides important information for those who are just arriving in the world of work.

i-uk – education

www.i-uk.com/education

A portal with advice and features about studying and living in the UK, with links to hundreds of institutions where you can get advice. It is aimed at a foreign audience but is extremely useful for UK students too.

Jobsearch

www.jobsearch.co.uk

Looking for a new job? You can search Jobsearch the website, post your CV and wait for the email replies. Employers can post their vacancies here too.

Lazy Student

www.lazystudent.co.uk

A comprehensive bundle of resources catering for all students' needs. There are good links to useful sites with a rating system. Everything is here at a click, from sports and music to money, culture and much more.

Learning and Skills Council

www.apprenticeships.org.uk

The Council offers opportunities to earn while you learn particular skills. It offers plenty of information and advice about specific skills and courses available in your area together with success stories from those who have taken part in schemes.

National Union of Students

www.nusonline.co.uk

An excellent website for students, and those about to go to university, with lots of news, information and practical advice about student life.

Open University

www.open.ac.uk

Website from the veteran in distance learning. The OU is the UK's largest university and accounts for 22 per cent of all part-time higher education students in the UK. The OU courses are considered to be amongst the best distance education materials in the world. Their website has full details of courses offered.

PAYAway

www.payaway.co.uk

This website offers practical advice and help for any young person thinking of taking work abroad whether for a gap year or a working holiday.

Prospects Street

www.prospects.co.uk/careers

An online careers service for 13–19 year olds. There is an online guided tour for finding a training course or exploring different career ideas or you take a psychometric course to find what career may best suit your competencies and personality.

Student

www.student.co.uk

Student.co.uk mixes entertainment and information. There are music and film reviews while topics such as money, travel, health and careers are covered regularly. You can join the debates on the busy message boards and win prizes in frequent competitions.

Student Loan Company

www.slc.co.uk

The website of the Student Loan Company who administer the student loans scheme. The website includes all of the latest news about student loans plus guidance on how they are administered along with repayment advice.

Student Money

www.studentmoney.org

Student money has helpful tools to plan and manage your student finance. The wage predictor tells you how much you'll earn while the loan repayment calculator looks into the amount of time you need to repay your student loan.

Student Radio Association

www.studentradio.org.uk

This association is the national representative body for student radio stations in the UK.

StudentUK

www.studentuk.com

An online advice and lifestyle magazine for students providing information, entertainment and services aimed at students. The website includes useful guides to managing cash, study, health, sport, accommodation and life after college.

StudentZone

www.studentzone.org.uk

Student Zone aims to meet the information needs of students, both on and off campus. The website sections include academic, careers, travel, legal, financial, health and entertainment.

Study UK

www.studyuk.hobsons.com

A useful site for foreign students coming to study in the UK with information on universities, colleges and short courses. It also covers matters such as lifestyle, the cost of living, the UK's travel network and legislation on UK education. Plus there is also a chatroom.

Support4Learning

www.support4learning.org.uk

A helpful site with extensive resources for everyone involved in education and training, covering areas such as choosing and financing education, training, career planning, lifelong learning and much more.

Teacher Training Agency

www.teach-tta.gov.uk

For students who are thinking of becoming teachers, this is a helpful and inspiring site.

TheSite

www.thesite.org.uk

With objective, impartial information and advice on issues such as health, relationships, careers, money, drugs and much more, TheSite aims to offer a 'guide to life' for young adults, aged 16 to 25.

The Student Room

www.thestudentroom.co.uk

A free, informal student discussion forum, run by students for students. You can follow the good online behaviour guidelines and dive into discussions about universities, schools, careers, and learning in general in one of the online forums.

UKCourseFinder

www.ukcoursefinder.com

A personal guide to higher education in the UK. You can just enter your interests, intentions and wishes and the site will find your dream course.

Universities and Colleges Admissions Service

www.ucas.co.uk

The website of the central organisation that processes applications for full-time undergraduate courses at universities and colleges in the UK. The first place to obtain information about studying in the UK, whether as a UK or foreign student.

Woman Student Online

www.womanstudent.co.uk

This website contains relevant and interesting information for women students, covering student life, health, money, careers, leisure and travel.

World-Wide Opportunities on Organic Farms (WWOOF)

www.wwoof.org

WWOOF aims to help those who would like to work as volunteers on organic farms around the world.

Year Out Group

www.yearoutgroup.org

The Year Out Group, backed by the DFES and UCAS, provides top-quality guidance and information about gap years and career breaks, helping young people (and their parents/advisers) to make the right choice of programme with the right

C 25

organisation. The member organisations of the group are rigorously vetted and monitored.

YMCA

www.ymca.org.uk

This website covers the work and aims of the YMCA which reaches out 'to young people, families and the community to help people grow in mind, body and spirit.' Follow the links to find YMCAs throughout the UK.

Young Enterprise

www.young-enterprise.org.uk

A website which encourages young people to learn more about business and the working environment while they are still at school or university. This site is also useful for teachers who may wish to incorporate YE's programmes to help them deliver their curriculum objectives.

Your Creative Future

www.yourcreativefuture.org

A really useful and colourful guide to education and career opportunities in the creative industries. Sponsored by the UK government, Design Council and Arts Council, the website has information and links to career information in creative sectors such as film, television and radio, design, fashion, architecture, music, new media, crafts, advertising, visual arts and much more.

Crafts and Hobbies

The internet can be an inspiration for those seeking ideas on how to make good use of their skills and spare time. In this category you will find websites covering a wide variety of crafts and hobbies – from badge collecting to gardening, digital photography to silk painting, and model railways to pottery, to name a few. **Further activities can be found in Sport and Activities, Dance, Drama and Theatre, Music, Art, and Internet Fun.**

4Car

About – Hobbies and Games

Aeroflight

All Crafts

Antiques Bulletin Online

Artcourses.co.uk

Badge Planet

BBC Gardening

Better Photo

British Journal of Photography

British Railway Modelling

Calligraphy and Lettering Arts Society

Car Net

Collecting Toy Soldiers

Crafts Council

Digital Photography Review

Docrafts

Drawing Power

Embroiderers' Guild

Flyer Air Portal

FreeFoto

Geoff's Woodwork

Guild of Silk Painters

Hornby

Internet Craft Fair

Joy of Shards Mosaics Resource

Knitting and Crochet Guild

Learn to Knit and Crochet

Living Heritage Craft Shows

Marquetry Society

Model Boats

Postcard Traders Association

Pottery Studio

Quilters' Guild

Robot Nut

Royal School of Needlework

Stanley Gibbons

Time to Learn

UK Model Shop Directory

UK Philately

UK Stained Glass News

Wargames Forum

Woodworking on the Web

Yahoo Hobbies

C 28

4Car

www.channel4.com/4car

The website for Channel 4's motoring show. It provides news, advice, reviews, features and chat.

About – Hobbies and Games

www.about.com/hobbies

A website providing links to a wide variety of hobby and game sites, divided into arts and crafts, collecting, electronic games, board games and pastimes.

Aeroflight

www.aeroflight.co.uk

A website that aims to be an 'authoritative information forum' for aviation enthusiasts.

All Crafts

www.allcrafts.net

This website offers tips and advice on a wide range of crafts including quilting, woodcraft, basketry, candle and soap making, crochet, knitting and much more. There are also free patterns and projects plus a big directory of arts and crafts links.

Antiques Bulletin Online

www.antiquesbulletin.co.uk

A website containing news from the world of antiques plus details of antique auctions, fairs, markets and centres as well as guidance on prices and valuations. This is a good site for anyone new to antiques.

Artcourses.co.uk

www.artcourses.co.uk

You can check on here for details of part-time classes, workshops and painting holidays. There are also helpful links to other art organisations, magazine sites and sites selling art materials.

Badge Planet

www.badgeplanet.co.uk

A website just for badge collectors and designers. They have a huge range of badges or you can design your own.

BBC Gardening

www.bbc.co.uk/gardening

A comprehensive site from the BBC with everything you may want to know about gardening. They also have a special 'gardening with children' section.

Better Photo

www.betterphoto.com

An online photography guide, suitable for both beginners and the more experienced, which aims to share photographic techniques and inspiration. They also offer a large number of online photography courses.

British Journal of Photography

www.bjphoto.co.uk

An online photography magazine. While the full site is available to subscribers only, there is still plenty here for non-subscribers, with lots of photography news, features and an extensive gallery.

British Railway Modelling

www.brmodelling.com

The online version of the monthly model railway magazine. This is a must visit website for model railway fans.

Calligraphy and Lettering Arts Society

www.clas.co.uk

A website promoting the beautiful artforms of calligraphy and lettering. CLAS promotes the study, practice and teaching of the artforms and on their website you can find details of courses, an events calendar, books and magazines and other resources.

Car Net

www.carnet.co.uk

The latest car news and features, reviews, details of motor shows and a photo gallery. The website also has sections on motoring laws and for learner drivers.

Collecting Toy Soldiers

www.toysoldier.freeuk.com

An extensive website, put together by a passionate collector, that will be a 'must visit' for all toy soldier fans.

Crafts Council

www.craftscouncil.org.uk

A website all about the aims and activities of the Crafts Council, which is the UK's national organisation for the promotion of contemporary crafts.

Digital Photography Review

www.dpreview.com

As digital photography becomes a popular hobby, this website is where you can find the latest news, reviews of the latest digital cameras, discussion forums, sample images and a buyers' guide.

Docrafts

www.docrafts.co.uk

This website is a 'source of creative inspiration' for card making, glass painting or rubber stamping with tips and projects plus it has a useful message board for posting all of your craft questions.

Drawing Power

www.drawingpower.org.uk

Get your pencils sharpened and start drawing! An ambitious website project that aims to get everybody drawing through involvement in projects and events.

C 29

Embroiderers' Guild

www.embroiderersguild.org.uk

The Embroiderers' Guild promotes the craft of embroidery. Their website provides details of their extensive products and services.

Flyer Air Portal

www.flyer.co.uk

An entertaining online magazine for everybody with an interest in flying.

FreeFoto

www.freefoto.com

This website offers a huge selection of good quality free pictures for private and non-commercial use.

Geoff's Woodwork

www.geoffswoodwork.co.uk

Created by a woodworking expert, this site provides helpful and practical resources about working with wood for both beginners and those seeking to improve their skills.

Guild of Silk Painters

www.silkpainters-guild.co.uk

You can increase your knowledge of silk painting or be inspired by the designs on display here at this website. The website can put you in contact with other artists who you can share your ideas and enthusiasm with.

Hornby

www.hornbyrailways.com

A website for everyone who wanted to grow up to be a train driver. Hornby is the most famous name in railway model making.

Internet Craft Fair

www.craft-fair.co.uk

An online guide to UK-made crafts with details of crafters, suppliers, craft guilds and organisations, craft events, magazines and courses.

Joy of Shards Mosaics Resource

www.thejoyofshards.co.uk

If you have ever considered making your own mosaics, this is a good website to start at. It contains step by step instructions to create your own, or alternatively you can check out mosaic masterpieces from around the world.

Knitting and Crochet Guild

www.knitting-and-crochet-guild.org.uk

A website detailing the work and activities of the Knitting and Crochet Guild, which promotes and encourages the crafts of hand-knitting, machine-knitting and crochet.

Learn to Knit and Crochet

www.learntoknit.com

A colourful US site for those learning how to knit and crochet, with projects and patterns plus links to other knitting sites and to knitting magazines.

Living Heritage Craft Shows

www.craft-show.co.uk

You can take time out to visit one of the craft shows listed on this website, see the artisans at work and enjoy lovely surroundings.

C 30

Marquetry Society

www.marquetry.org

Marquetry is an interesting craft that combines artistic imagination with great skill. Have a look on this website at what can be done by visiting the gallery and learning more about this technique which involves covering an entire surface of a board or piece of furniture with a veneer in the form of a skillfully applied design or picture. The website contains simple instructions on how to make a chessboard and other creative crafts.

Model Boats

www.modelboats.co.uk

An online magazine for model boat enthusiasts, with lots of news and features. There is also an online modelshop and forum.

Postcard Traders Association

www.postcard.co.uk

The website of the Postcard Traders Association is a must for postcard collectors and those thinking of taking up the hobby.

Pottery Studio

www.studiopottery.com

An attractive and informative website that will be of interest to collectors, students and lovers of all kinds of pottery. It offers a good insight into the history of pottery with plenty of illustrations.

Quilters' Guild

www.quiltersguild.org.uk

The Quilters' Guild promotes the art of quilting. Their website has details of events, online quilting projects and a wealth of information related to this craft.

Robot Nut

www.robotnut.com

A great archive containing toy robot images, a history of toy robots and galleries featuring 1960's space toys and classic robots.

Royal School of Needlework

www.royal-needlework.co.uk

The Royal School of Needlework has taught the traditional art of hand embroidery for over 130 years. You can find out here about their classes, courses and events.

Stanley Gibbons

www.stanleygibbons.com

This is undoubtedly the most famous name in philately. Their website is a must-visit for all stamp collectors.

Time to Learn

www.timetolearn.org.uk

This website provides a useful collection of courses from City and Guilds giving you the opportunity to explore your creativity, develop new skills and have fun.

UK Model Shop Directory

www.ukmodelshops.co.uk

This is not just a directory of model shops. It also provides details of clubs, exhibitions and railway attractions. It is a 'one stop shop' for everything related to model railways.

UK Philately

www.ukphilately.org.uk

An excellent website both for newcomers to stamp collecting and experienced philatelists. The website includes a special area for the young philatelist.

UK Stained Glass News

www.stainedglassnews.co.uk

An online magazine dedicated to the art of stained glass, featuring stunning stained glass artwork. The website also has many good patterns and recommendations about places to visit.

Wargames Forum

www.wargames.co.uk

An extensive war games site that includes news, reviews and clubs plus it has links to relevant trading and book sites.

Woodworking on the Web

www.woodworking.co.uk

Beginners and experienced alike can meet in this virtual space and share tips and ideas about woodturning, furniture making and woodcarving.

Yahoo Hobbies

www.yahoo.co.uk/recreation/ hobbies

Yahoo has links to websites that cover a huge range of hobbies.

Dance

This category contains dance news, reviews, guides, schools, companies, courses, magazines, books, auditions, history – and much more. The sites included here cover every form of dance from ballet to modern. Whether you wish to follow a career in dance, are interested in dancing just for fun, or prefer to admire the skills of professional dancers, the internet can help improve your knowledge and understanding of this art form. **Visit Drama and Theatre, Film, Television and Radio and the Music categories for other related sites.**

Ballet.co.uk

BBC Blast Dance

Ceroc

Choreograph.net

Circus Space

Constellation Change Screen Dance Festival

Council for Dance Education and Training

Crictical Dance

CyberDance

Dance Europe

Dance Links

Dance Music Resource

Dance Network

Dance UK

Dance Umbrella

DanceWeb

Dancing Times

Dolmetsch Historical Dance Society

English Amateur Dance Sport Association

English Folk Dance and Song Society

Fizzycool

Imperial Society of Teachers of Dancing

International Dance Sport Federation

International Dance Teachers Association

KFA Youth Moves

Language of Dance Centre

London Dance

National Resource Centre for Dance

The Place

Royal Academy of Dance

Royal Ballet

Salsa and Merengue

UK Line Dancing

Young Dancers

Ballet.co.uk

www.ballet.co.uk

A comprehensive guide to all things ballet and dance in the world, but dealing in depth with the UK. The website contains reviews, news, links, ballet and dance companies, information on performers, listings of ballet schools and multiple links.

BBC Blast Dance

www.bbc.co.uk/blast/dance

From circus skills to contemporary dance to fire performance – get support, ideas and advice from this inspiring site. The sections include a chatroom, message board, ask an expert, dancefloor, dance map, careers and links.

Ceroc

www.ceroc.com

Ceroc is a fusion of jive and salsa. Ceroc is easy to learn and it is the fastest growing partner dance in the UK. The Ceroc website will tell you where you can find classes. Ceroc is primarily social and fun and it keeps you fit!

Choreograph.net

www.choreograph.net

A website dedicated to contemporary choreography, dance and culture, providing a forum for artists and choreographers.

Circus Space

www.thecircusspace.co.uk

The Circus Space is a centre of excellence in the circus arts, offering support and services for professional performers, aspiring performers, adults and young people in the circus arts.

Constellation Change Screen Dance Festival

www.constellation-change.co.uk

This website contains award winning dance on film. The entries include everyone from students to professionals.

Council for Dance Education and Training

www.cdet.org.uk

The council promotes excellence in dance education and training. It offers support and advice to students, parents, teachers and artists and provides a comprehensive information service.

Critical Dance

www.criticaldance.com

A website dedicated to ballet, modern dance and all forms of performance dance. It houses comprehensive site listings of schools, courses, presenters, publications, reviews, photos and all things dance worldwide, with a useful country by country search engine facility.

CyberDance

www.cyberdance.org

A US directory containing over 3,500 links to modern dance and classical ballet pages on the internet.

Dance Europe

www.danceeurope.net

An entertaining and colourful online dance magazine with features, auditions, news, reviews, links, courses and much more.

Dance Links

**www.dancer.com/
dance-links/schools.htm**

A worldwide and UK directory of dance schools.

Dance Music Resource

www.juno.co.uk

This website claims to be the world's largest dance music store. Juno Records has over 36,000 titles in stock including garage, hip-hop/r&b, techno, trance plus many more genres to choose from.

Dance Network

www.dancenetwork.org.uk

A website developed by the National Dance Teachers Association, the Specialist Schools Trust and the Youth Sport Trust. It is supported by the Department for Education and Skills and the Arts Council to help develop and promote all areas of dance. There are good links here.

Dance UK

www.danceuk.org

Working 'with and on behalf of dance', the Dance UK website provides information, publications, networks and forums for debate. It is a unified voice speaking on behalf of the profession.

Dance Umbrella

www.danceumbrella.co.uk

Dance Umbrella is devoted to celebrating and championing contemporary dance and it is dedicated to the development of choreography, choreographers and dancers.

DanceWeb

www.danceweb.co.uk

A huge interactive directory for all UK dancing enthusiasts and most dance styles. The website provides help with finding a dance class, school, product, web resource and much more.

Dancing Times

www.dancing-times.co.uk

The home of the Dancing Times and Dance Today magazines plus it provides links and information on books, reviews and articles on all forms of dance.

Dolmetsch Historical Dance Society

www.dhds.org.uk

The DHDS promotes understanding of the theory and practice of European dance from the twelfth to the nineteenth century.

English Amateur Dance Sport Association

www.eada.org.uk

The governing body for amateur competitive dancesport, the EADA provides support, advice and training for amateur dancers at all levels.

English Folk Dance and Song Society

www.efdss.org

For over 100 years, the Society has acted to preserve and promote the traditional song and dance of England.

Fizzycool

www.fizzycool.org.uk

A teacher-training provider in dance and drama. You can learn here how to become an inspirational, effective and safe teacher.

Imperial Society of Teachers of Dancing

www.istd.org

An informative site about the work of the ISTD, which is the world's leading dance examinations board. Its aim is to 'educate the public in the art of dancing in all its forms', mainly through maintaining and improving teaching standards and qualifying teachers through examinations.

International Dance Sport Federation

www.idsf.net

The aim of the International DanceSport Federation is to promote dancesport internationally and to advise and assist its members with their work in their own countries.

International Dance Teachers Association

www.idta.co.uk

The IDTA provides a diverse range of activities for and on behalf of teachers including training, tuition, seminars and support programmes. Their work covers the broadest range of dance disciplines.

KFA Youth Moves

www.keepfit.org.uk/youthmoves. htm

KFA Youth Moves is aimed at children up to age 16 and it is the perfect route to fitness through movement, exercise and dance.

Language of Dance Centre

www.lodc.org.

Based on the 'movement alphabet', the Language of Dance Centre's aim is to teach dance through appreciation, interpretation, evaluation of material and observation.

London Dance

www.londondance.com

A round up of dance in the capital with previews, reviews, listings and dance related television and radio plus it provides links to associated directories and much more.

National Resource Centre for Dance

www.surrey.ac.uk/NRCD

The NRCD aims to preserve the nation's dance heritage and enables, supports, and enhances the study and teaching of dance.

The Place

www.theplace.org.uk

'The Place' to learn dance, discover dance, watch dance, create dance and debate dance. That is contemporary dance in every form.

Royal Academy of Dance

www.rad.org.uk

The Royal Academy of Dance promotes the knowledge, understanding and practice of dance. It promotes drama, educates and trains both students and dance teachers and manages examinations.

D 36

Royal Ballet

www.royalballet.org

A website detailing what's on at the Royal Ballet, how to buy tickets for events and how to make the most of your visit.

Salsa and Merengue

www.salsa-merengue.co.uk

The Salsa and Merengue Society offers the opportunity to learn more about dance and Latin culture and has links to classes, events and teachers.

UK Line Dancing

www.uk-linedancingdirectory.co.uk

This is a selected directory of line dancing websites.

Young Dancers

www.young-dancers.org

An attractive dance website just for teenagers providing photos, what's on, career information and advice on why, what and where to learn. It covers all forms of dance.

Drama and Theatre

There are many sites here that will be of interest to fans of the dramatic arts and those studying drama, as well as information for theatre-goers. In addition to theatre guides and details of drama festivals, there are websites covering everything from amateur dramatics to Shakespeare's play, sites for children and teenagers, and guidance for those wishing to pursue a career in drama whether this is in acting, backstage or as a playwright. **You will find related sites under Dance, Film, Television and Radio, Music, English and Media.**

Amdram

Andrew McCann's Drama Workshop

Arts Council England

Conference of Drama Schools

Connect

Culture Online

Dance and Drama Awards

Drama in Education

Edinburgh Fringe

Ents 24

Equity

Guide to Musical Theatre

Independent Radio Drama Productions

London Theatre Guide

London Theatre Guide Online

National Association of Youth Theatres

National Council for Drama Training

National Museum of the Performing Arts

National Student Drama Festival

National Theatre

Plays on the Net

Royal Academy of Dramatic Art

Royal Shakespeare Company

SchoolPlay Productions

Scottish Arts Council

Shakespeare's Monologues

Society of Teachers of Speech and Drama

Stage

Stagework

TheatreNet

UK Theatre Web

Virtual Drama Studio

Virtual Library Theatre and Drama

Whatsonstage

Youth Arts Online

Amdram

www.amdram.co.uk

This is a website for anyone interested in amateur dramatics. It is a friendly, informative and useful resource network.

Andrew McCann's Drama Workshop

www.dramateachers.co.uk

A website offering good advice from Andrew, a drama teacher, who compiled this useful bank of information and resources to improve drama students' performance results.

Arts Council England

www.arts.org.uk

The national development agency for the arts, Arts Council England invests public funds in the arts in England, including funding from the National Lottery.

Conference of Drama Schools

www.drama.ac.uk

Comprising the UK's 21 leading drama schools, CDS maintains the highest standards of training within the vocational drama sector, thus making it easier for prospective students to understand the range of courses on offer. The website provides links to principle drama and theatre establishments throughout the UK.

Connect

http://connect.gsmd.ac.uk

This website is from the Guildhall School of Music and Drama. Connect offers participants from a range of communities – some local, others drawn from around the globe – the chance to take part in high quality cross-arts and trans-cultural music projects. The Connect philosophy embraces everything from classical to pop music and is inspired by western and non-western genres.

Culture Online

www.cultureonline.gov.uk

An initiative from the Department of Culture, Media and Sport to increase access to, and participation in, arts and culture. It brings together cultural organisations to create projects that will delight adults and children of all ages.

Dance and Drama Awards

www.dfes.gov.uk/financialhelp/ dancedrama

Information is available on this website about the government's dance and drama awards for students (16+) who want to become professional actors, dancers or stage managers.

Drama in Education

www.kentaylor.co.uk/die

This site, established by a drama lecturer, is a great resource and was developed to support teachers who use drama in education.

Edinburgh Fringe

www.edfringe.com

An informative site explaining what is on at the Fringe at the annual Edinburgh Festival.

Ents 24

www.ents24.com

A wide-ranging and comprehensive entertainment guide covering what's on in film, theatre, comedy, music and festivals around the UK.

Equity

www.equity.org.uk

Equity is the trade union representing artists and performers across the entertainment spectrum including directors, choreographers, stage designers and others working behind the scenes. Their website also contains a directory of children's entertainers.

Guide to Musical Theatre

www.nodanw.com

Developed for those who enjoy musicals, the website for Guide to Musical Theatre provides a comprehensive listing of musical shows. There is also an online guide to books about the theatre.

Independent Radio Drama Productions

www.irdp.co.uk

One of the world's leading independent producers of radio drama, IRDP promotes drama on radio and provides opportunities for writers new to the medium.

London Theatre Guide

www.officiallondontheatre.co.uk

The Society of London Theatre's comprehensive guide to shows in London's theatreland. It has a great section for children and young people.

London Theatre Guide Online

www.londontheatre.co.uk

A reliable and comprehensive guide to what's on at theatres across London.

National Association of Youth Theatres

www.nayt.org.uk

The work of the NAYT supports the development of youth theatre activity through training, advocacy and participation programmes.

National Council for Drama Training

www.ncdt.co.uk

A professional body overseeing drama training and providing quality assurance and accreditation.

National Museum of the Performing Arts

www.theatremuseum.org

The National Museum of the Performing Arts houses unique collections, recordings and archives plus information on activities to support teachers in the delivery of the national curriculum and to trigger the interest of pupils in the performing arts.

National Student Drama Festival

www.nsdf.org.uk

The annual National Student Drama Festival brings students and leading theatre professionals together and showcases live, enterprising theatre by young people.

National Theatre

www.nt-online.org

A guide to shows and plays at the National Theatre in London.

D40

Plays on the Net

www.playsonthenet.com

Fancy yourself as a playwright? On this website you can submit your own play, or read and comment on plays sent in by others.

Royal Academy of Dramatic Art

www.rada.org

The world-renowned RADA provides actors and technicians with training of the highest quality.

Royal Shakespeare Company

www.rsc.org.uk

The aim of the RSC is to 'keep audiences in touch with Shakespeare' and maintain an understanding of his work through artists, actors and writers. Find out on this website what's on and where.

SchoolPlay Productions

www.schoolplayproductions.co.uk

SchoolPlay Productions Limited was founded in 1989 to promote school plays and musicals for performance for youth groups and schools.

Scottish Arts Council

www.scottisharts.org.uk

Championing the arts in Scotland, the Scottish Arts Council channels public funds, and National Lottery money, into the arts in Scotland.

Shakespeare's Monologues

www.shakespeare-monologues.org

This website contains comprehensive, well-researched and easy-to-find listings of all Shakespeare's monologues.

Society of Teachers of Speech and Drama

www.stsd.org.uk

This international organisation encourages good standards of teaching for every form of speech and dramatic art and also brings together drama students and teachers.

Stage

www.thestage.co.uk

The online version of the famous entertainment magazine, first published in 1880. It is essential reading for anyone interested in showbusiness.

Stagework

www.stagework.org.uk

Managed by the National Theatre, Stagework aims to improve understanding of theatre as a creative industry and to open up career opportunities for young people. The website offers curriculum resources for teachers and learners of English, drama, citizenship and other subjects.

TheatreNet

www.theatrenet.com

An attractive and informative guide to London theatre.

UK Theatre Web

www.uktw.co.uk

This is a lively site for theatre fans. It includes sections on amateur dramatics and chat as well as theatre information.

Virtual Drama Studio

www.thevirtualdramastudio.co.uk

A website providing recommended resource and lesson plans for teachers helping to improve the learning experience for 11 to 18 year old theatre and drama students.

Virtual Library Theatre and Drama

www.vl-theatre.com

An extensive directory that contains links to drama and theatre resources around the world. The website provides plays in print, theatre studies, costume and much more. It is aimed at academics, amateurs, professionals and students.

Whatsonstage

www.whatsonstage.com

A comprehensive guide to what's on stage in the UK providing news, views, reviews and features.

Youth Arts Online

www.youthartsonline.org

Youth Arts Online is a new website for anyone under 26 who enjoys the arts and wants to get involved. Their site has loads of information including addresses, workshops, courses and more. It covers dance, drama, music, singing, visual arts, creative writing, new media, television, radio, film, video, carnival, circus and crafts.

Education and Teachers

This category covers a wide range of subjects and resources for teachers and those interested in all aspects of educational news and debate, the National Curriculum, academic and vocational qualifications, ICT in schools, the International Baccalaureate, literacy, government policy, educational shows, E-credits and much more. **National Curriculum subjects will be found under the individual curriculum categories, e.g. English, Geography, Maths, etc. See also Information Technology, Special Needs, and Parents and Guardians for related sites.**

Artscape

Association of Teachers Websites

British Educational Communications and
  Technology Agency

Chalkface.Net

Curriculum Online

Department for Culture, Media and Sport

Department for Education and Skills

Development Education Association

Echalk.co.uk

Edexcel

Educate the Children

Education Marketplace

Education Place

English and Media Centre

English Online

Geography Online

Good Typing

Guardian Education

History Online

ICT Teachers

Interactive Resources

International Baccalaureate Organization

JANET Higher Education Administration

Kidsmart

Learn.co.uk

LearnDirect

Learning and Teaching Scotland

Learning Curve

Learnpremium

London Association for the Teaching of English

London Schools Arts Services

MathSphere

MirandaNet

National Association for Literature Development

National Association for the Teaching of English

National Association of Writers in Education

National Grid For Learning

National Literacy Strategy

OCR

Primary Worksheets

Qualifications and Curriculum Authority

Red Box

SAM Learning

Schools Fantasy League

Schools Net

Science Online

Scottish Qualifications Authority

Teacher Support Network

Teaching Awards

Teaching Ideas for Primary Teachers

TEEM

Times Educational Supplement

Tools for Schools

Wired For Health

Young NCB

E 44

Artscape

www.artscape.org.uk

A directory featuring organisations and artists who undertake work in education, both in the formal sector and within the community.

Association of Teachers Websites

www.byteachers.org.uk

A website containing useful educational sites for teachers, pupils and parents, plus a 'virtual school' with a range of online lessons.

British Educational Communications and Technology Agency

www.becta.org.uk

BECTA is the government's key partner in the strategic development and delivery of its ICT and e-learning strategy for the schools, learning and skills sectors. The website contains links for teachers, ICT links for schools and pupils, ICT awards and the latest news and facts about ICT in education.

Chalkface.Net

www.chalkface.net

Chalkface net is an 'ISP portal and educational resource centre for teachers, by teachers.' This thoroughly comprehensive and useful website provides worksheets, downloadable lessons and valuable information with links for primary through to secondary subjects including DT, Languages and Maths.

Curriculum Online

www.curriculumonline.gov.uk

On here you will find the definitive list of multimedia resources that your school can buy with its eLC money. All the resources here are geared to the subjects taught in schools in the UK. It is a good place to search for online multimedia resources for any subject that is part of the national curriculum.

Department for Culture, Media and Sport

www.culture.gov.uk

The DCMS is responsible for government policy in areas such as the arts, sport, tourism, libraries, museums, galleries and broadcasting. There are facts, figures and reports on the website showing how the government is working in these areas.

Department for Education and Skills

www.dfes.gov.uk

The DfES aims to give children an excellent start in education, equip young people with life and work skills and encourage adults to realise their potential through learning. Good resources are available on the site for teachers.

Development Education Association

www.dea.org.uk

The DEA aims to raise awareness and understanding of how global issues affect the lives of individuals, communities and societies – and how we influence the society we live in. It aims to bring global perspectives into all aspects of learning.

Echalk.co.uk

www.echalk.co.uk

This website is a free resource for teachers to use with interactive whiteboards and data projectors. An impressive and excellent tool for primary and secondary Science and Maths teachers using interactive whiteboards.

Edexcel

www.edexcel.org.uk

Edexcel is a leading provider of academic and vocational qualifications, including GCSEs, AS and A levels, GNVQs, BTEC First, National, and Higher National Certificates and Diplomas, NVQs, Key Skills and Entry Qualifications and specific programmes for employers.

Educate the Children

www.educate.org.uk

An excellent resource for primary teachers, parents and schools. All subjects are given comprehensive coverage and there are links to work sheets and interactive class room activities.

Education Marketplace

www.education-marketplace.co.uk

Education Marketplace contains links to websites for the UK's leading educational resource shows and events: BETT, SETT, the Education Show, Special Needs London, Education Show London and Education Marketplace magazine.

Education Place

www.eduplace.com

A website containing K-8 resources for teachers, students, and parents. It includes reading, language, maths,

E 45

science, social studies, intervention, professional development, activities, games, and textbook support.

English and Media Centre

www.englishandmedia.co.uk

The English and Media Centre serves the needs of secondary and FE teachers and students of English and media studies through training courses, publications for the classroom and magazines for A level students.

English Online

www.englishonline.co.uk

English Online provides teaching materials for all stages of secondary education including lesson plans and interactive units.

Geography Online

www.geographyonline.co.uk

A subscription website supporting geography teachers with constantly expanding resources across the geography curriculum.

Good Typing

www.goodtyping.com

A free online typing course in 27 guided lessons.

Guardian Education

http://education.guardian.co.uk

The Guardian website's education pages will keep you up to date with all the latest education news, covering all aspects of the subject.

History Online

www.historyonline.co.uk

A subscription resource for history teachers containing high quality stand-alone lessons, materials, sourcebooks and more.

ICT Teachers

www.icteachers.co.uk

This is a useful resource and provides links for teachers and parents.

Interactive Resources

www.interactive-resources.co.uk

A variety of maths resources are available from the Interactive Resources website.

International Baccalaureate Organization

www.ibo.org

This is the homepage of the International Baccalaureate Organization and it explains in detail the increasingly popular 'IB' educational programmes.

JANET Higher Education Administration

www.sbu.ac.uk/juga

A directory site with links relating to higher education for use by administrators. It includes HE funding and administration and a complete list of university and college websites.

Kidsmart

www.kidsmart.org.uk

A practical internet safety advice website for schools. The site focuses on 5 key SMART safety tips such as what children need to remember when they use the internet or mobile phone.

Learn.co.uk

www.learn.co.uk

This educational website from the Guardian that aims to 'support, stimulate and succeed'. It provides lessons in support of the national curriculum, resources for learners and online activities.

LearnDirect

www.learndirect.co.uk

A network of online learning and information services, offering courses in three main categories: skills for life (including literacy and numeracy), business, management and IT skills.

Learning and Teaching Scotland

www.scet.org.uk

LT Scotland provides support, resources and staff development for early years and school education in Scotland, and promotes learning throughout life. It supports development in learning and education, including the use of ICT.

Learning Curve

www.learningcurve.pro.gov.uk

An online teaching resource that ties in with the history national curriculum from key stages 2 to 5. From the National Archives, it uses a range of original sources including documents, photographs, film and sound recordings.

Learnpremium

www.learnpremium.co.uk

LearnPremium covers reception through to AS level and is presented in the national curriculum's key stages. A yearly subscription allows unlimited access by teachers and pupils to all areas of the site.

Plus, learnpremium can be paid for with e-learning credits. An extremely well laid out and easy to navigate system, covering all subjects for all ages.

London Association for the Teaching of English

www.late.org.uk

Members of LATE include teachers from primary, secondary, further education, advisers, consultants, teacher trainers and student teachers. All are concerned with English teaching and language development.

London Schools Arts Services

www.lonsas.org.uk

This is the one-stop shop for London schools and colleges interested in creative arts projects and arts partnerships. It offers initiatives and awards across the disciplines of dance, music, drama, theatre, etc.

MathSphere

www.mathsphere.co.uk

Samples of MathSphere's software, designed to improve primary school children's knowledge of mathematics using straightforward worksheets, are available to view here. Other topics covered include fractions, squares, cubes and geometry. There is also a free teacher's resource for use in the classroom.

MirandaNet

www.mirandanet.ac.uk

The MirandaNet Fellowship aims to further the development of educators who are meeting the challenge of advanced technologies in classrooms.

National Association for Literature Development

www.nald.org

This website provides a list of members plus news and information about developments in literature and the arts.

National Association for the Teaching of English

www.nate.org.uk

NATE conducts research into the teaching of English and is involved in curriculum development initiatives with the Arts Council and the National Council for Educational Technology.

National Association of Writers in Education

www.nawe.co.uk

NAWE supports the development of creative writing in all educational settings throughout the UK.

National Grid For Learning

www.ngfl.gov.uk

This is the government's 'gateway to educational resources on the internet'. You should visit this site regularly for up to the minute information on the latest education news and features and for links to educational websites with quality information and content.

National Literacy Strategy

www.standards.dfes.gov.uk/literacy

The National Literacy Strategy supports teachers, trainee teachers and others working to improve literacy in primary schools.

OCR

www.ocr.org.uk

The work and services provided by OCR, one of the UK's leading awards bodies. They provide qualifications to students at schools, colleges, in part-time learning and in work.

Primary Worksheets

www.primaryworksheets.co.uk

This website contains extensive primary level worksheets plus links to related sites.

Qualifications and Curriculum Authority

www.qca.org.uk

A website all about the important work of the QCA, which maintains and develops the national curriculum and associated tests and examinations. It also accredits and monitors qualifications in colleges and at work.

Red Box

www.redbox.gov.uk

A clever interactive resource that teaches pupils about tax and public spending. It contains two sites, for 7–11 year olds and 11–16 year olds.

SAM Learning

www.samlearning.co.uk

A website providing comprehensive online learning courses for SATs, GCSEs and A levels which is currently used by over 2,000 schools in the UK. The courses are proven to raise achievement.

Schools Fantasy League

www.schoolsfl.com

The game that helps pupils build cross-curriculum skills through fantasy football. This fun, educational football management game, which is based on the real performance of Premiership players, helps students develop skills in ICT, mathematics, science, English, business studies and citizenship.

Schools Net

www.schoolsnet.com

A website providing links to schools in all areas, and inviting teachers to use the education community where they can share knowledge and experience with others. This site is an excellent learning and revision resource for students and teachers. It provides current GCSE and primary lessons plus revision papers across all subjects.

Science Online

www.scienceonline.co.uk

A subscription website with a constantly expanding range of resources for science teachers.

Scottish Qualifications Authority

www.sqa.org.uk

SQA is the national body in Scotland responsible for the development, accreditation, assessment and certification of qualifications other than degrees.

Teacher Support Network

www.teachersupport.org.uk

The work of the Teacher Support Network which provides support to teachers and lecturers, both serving and retired, and their families.

Teaching Awards

www.teachingawards.com

A website all about the Teaching Awards, which celebrate excellence and promote best practice in education.

Teaching Ideas for Primary Teachers

www.teachingideas.co.uk

An excellent resource for primary school teachers covering all national curriculum subjects with colourful, interactive work sheets to make the learning more fun.

TEEM

www.teem.org.uk

An informative site giving guidance for teachers and parents on the suitability of educational software. The site contains all of the latest programmes and online reviews.

Times Educational Supplement

www.tes.co.uk

The online version of the Times Educational Supplement, with the latest news on education issues, features, archives, and everything to keep teachers in touch with the latest in the profession.

Tools for Schools

www.tfs.org.uk

A website offering companies a solution for disposing of their computers. Tools for Schools matches computers that companies no longer require with schools that need them.

Wired For Health

www.wiredforhealth.gov.uk

Wired for Health provides information for parents, teachers and health and education professionals relating to the health of children and young people.

Young NCB

www.youngncb.org.uk

Young NCB is a free membership network for children and young people, run by the National Children's Bureau. There is lots of information here on issues of direct relevance to youngsters – the site has two sections, one for primary users and one for teenagers.

E 50

English

Here you will find websites covering English for GCSE, AS and A Level, English literature, reading resources, online teachers, support, grammar, spelling, study notes and guides, vocabulary aids, online dictionaries, thesaurus, digital texts, virtual libraries and more. **The Reference and Revision categories as well as Media and Drama and Theatre also provide useful learning tools and support for students and teachers of this all-important subject.**

Alex Catalogue of Electronic Texts

AllDictionaries

Anagram Genius

Andrew Moore's Teaching Resource Site

AntiStudy

Ask Oxford

Author Co Uk

Bibliomania

Booktrust

Channel 4 Book Box

Cool-reads

Dictionary.com

Encyclopaedia Britannica

English Association

English Resources

English Teaching in the UK

Englishbiz

FRET

Fun With Words

GCSE Revision – English

International Library of Poetry

Invisible Ink

iSciFiStory

Jane Austen Information Page

Kids' Review

Literary Encyclopedia

Litnotes UK

Luminarium

Merriam-Webster Online

National Literacy Strategy

National Literary Trust

National Reading Campaign

New Writer

Novelguide

OneLook Dictionary Search

OnLine Books Page

Online Library of Literature

Perseus Digital Library

Poetry Book Society

Project Gutenberg

Quoteland

Reading is Fundamental, UK

RhymeZone

Shake Sphere

Shakespeare Online

ShakespeareHelp

Teachit

Thesaurus

Web English Teacher

Word Detective

World Book Day

Worldwide Words

Young Writer

E 52

Alex Catalogue of Electronic Texts

www.infomotions.com/alex

An indexed collection of classic American and English literature that is in the public domain.

AllDictionaries

www.alldictionaries.com

A directory of dictionaries with links to more than 800 dictionary sites covering a variety of languages and a wide range of subjects.

Anagram Genius

www.anagramgenius.com

This site allows you to search for anagrams. Run a name through the anagram finder and it will be transformed – though not always for the better.

Andrew Moore's Teaching Resource Site

www.universalteacher.org.uk

Written by an English teacher, this site has comprehensive and well structured resources for teachers and students of English language and literature.

AntiStudy

www.antistudy.com

Search engine for free book notes and literature study notes online. A good starting point if you have a book title and want to find out more about it. Covers over 500 novels, poems and plays. Visit this site for text from Great Expectations, Catcher in the Rye, Pride and Prejudice, and many others.

Ask Oxford

www.askoxford.com

Oxford Dictionaries are passionate about language. This site offers a word of the day, quotes from well known books, tips on writing, an Ask the Experts section and a useful global English section.

Author Co Uk

www.author.co.uk

A website providing book reviews and a wealth of information about authors and their work along with advice about writing your own masterpiece, an e-zine and a broad range of services.

Bibliomania

www.bibliomania.com

This website provides free online literature with over 2,000 classic texts, literature book notes, authors' biographies, book summaries, reference books, study guides and much more.

Booktrust

www.booktrust.org.uk

'Bringing books and readers together'. Booktrust's website contains recommended titles, reading lists, lists of childrens' bookshops, book organisations, authors' sites, book prizes, projects and lots more to encourage readers of all ages and cultures to discover and enjoy books.

Channel 4 Book Box

www.channel4.com/bookbox

Information about popular writers and their books is available on this colourful and interactive site that encourages 9 to 13 year olds to read. There are also games and activities available, and a writing toolkit to stimulate creative writing.

Cool-reads

www.cool-reads.co.uk

A brilliant site where books for 10–15 year olds are reviewed by other 10–15 year olds. Over 2,500 books have been reviewed, split into more than 30 categories.

Dictionary.com

www.dictionary.com

This website contains a multi-source dictionary search facility. Simply type in the word and the site will look up the word in several dictionaries at once and provide a definition.

Encyclopaedia Britannica

www.britannica.co.uk

The website housing the Encyclopaedia Britannica. You can buy the complete set of books here.

English Association

www.le.ac.uk/engassoc

A website all about the work of the English Association, which aims to further the knowledge, enjoyment and understanding of English language and literature and to foster good practice in its learning and teaching.

English Resources

www.englishresources.co.uk

Free English language and literature teaching and revision resources for 11 to 18 year olds are available on this website.

English Teaching in the UK

www.english1.org.uk

The approved content provider for the National Grid for Learning maintained by Harry Dodds, Head of English at Gosfield School. This site is a forum for teachers of English to gather and share ideas, resources and useful links.

Englishbiz

www.englishbiz.co.uk

A website providing English and English literature help and revision guides for GCSE students, concentrating on the key skills you need. Your suggestions and feedback are also welcome as the site's content is regularly updated.

FRET

www.englishteaching.co.uk

A site providing teaching resources, lesson plans and schemes of work exclusively for English teachers. It is organised according to the national curriculum and covers reading, writing, listening and speaking at each key stage.

Fun With Words

www.fun-with-words.com

This website is dedicated to the oddities and peculiarities of the English language. It has more palindromes, spoonerisms, oxymorons, mnemonics and malapropisms than you can shake a stick at.

GCSE Revision – English

www.gcse.com/english/index.htm

The material being developed for this site will help all GCSE students with their English revision.

International Library of Poetry

www.poetry.com

Thousands of poems are posted on this US site by amateur poets, along with classic poets and their work. The site contains competitions, help and resources to encourage and stimulate the poet in all of us.

Invisible Ink

www.invink.com

On this website you can read reviews and excerpts from more than 500 ghostly titles from around the world on this US site. You can learn how to write your own ghost book and get information on where to find ghost stories and a bibliography.

iSciFiStory

www.iscifistory.com

This website contains writing exercises for those with a passion and yearning for sci-fi and fantasy writing.

Jane Austen Information Page

www.pemberley.com/janeinfo/ janeinfo.html

A huge store of information about the work and writing of Jane Austen is available from this website.

Kids' Review

www.kidsreview.org.uk

An educational, challenging and safe website where children are encouraged in their reading and writing by reviewing the books they have enjoyed reading.

Literary Encyclopedia

www.litencyc.com

The Literary Encyclopedia and Literary Dictionary website provides profiles of the lives and works of literary authors whose works are valued in the English language, together with profiles of prominent figures such as philosophers and musicians.

Litnotes UK

www.litnotes.co.uk

A website offering free resources for AS/A2 level English language, English literature and media studies.

Luminarium

www.luminarium.org.

An award-winning site with comprehensive material on medieval, renaissance and

E 54

17th century English literature. Entire texts can be downloaded from this site.

Merriam-Webster Online

www.m-w.com

A fine general US-English dictionary and thesaurus. Features online dictionaries for bi-lingual and specialist English words, word games and a special section for kids.

National Literacy Strategy

www.standards.dfes.gov.uk/ literacy

From the DfES, the National Literacy Strategy website supports teachers and others who are working to improve literacy in primary schools. There is guidance available here about strategy along with updates about initiatives and events that support literacy.

National Literary Trust

www.literacytrust.org.uk

Recognising that literacy is central to economic advance and the development of human potential, this trust is dedicated to raising litaracy standards for all age groups throughout the UK.

National Reading Campaign

www.yearofreading.org.uk

Delivered by the National Literacy Trust, the National Reading Campaign promotes reading throughout the community. A website for people of all ages and abilities.

New Writer

www.thenewwriter.com

An online magazine for writers and authors aspiring to be published. You can follow their guidelines and submit your own work.

Novelguide

www.novelguide.com

This website is a free source of literary analysis. Novelguide is a US site that provides an educational supplement for the better understanding of classic and contemporary literature.

OneLook Dictionary Search

www.onelook.com

A search engine for words and phrases. Over 5 million words in more than 900 online dictionaries are indexed here. On this website you can define, translate or find words.

OnLine Books Page

www.digital.library.upenn.edu/ books

A website facilitating access to books that are freely readable over the internet. An index of thousands of free online books and pointers to directories and archives of online texts.

Online Library of Literature

www.literature.org/authors

This website provides full and unabridged texts of classic works of English literature. The site is under continuous development and encourages readers to make suggestions about any work they would like to see added.

Perseus Digital Library

www.perseus.tufts.edu

If you are interested in, or studying, the Classics you will find a wide range of source material on this site including texts, translations, art and archaeology.

Poetry Book Society

www.poetrybooks.co.uk

On this website, the best poetry books are reviewed and offered to members of the society at discounted prices.

Project Gutenberg

www.promo.net/pg

You can find on this website the complete text of thousands of books whose copyrights are now in the public domain including classic books from the nineteenth and early twentieth centuries.

Quoteland

www.quoteland.com

Search on this website for quotes by subject or person. Whether you are seeking words of wisdom or a line for an essay or speech, you will find the quote you need here.

Reading is Fundamental, UK

www.rif.org.uk

From the National Literacy Trust comes this wonderful site that encourages all young people to take up reading. The projects here make reading fun, fun, fun.

RhymeZone

www.rhymezone.com

Become an instant poet! Just type in your word and let this site find relevant rhymes, synonyms and definitions.

Shake Sphere

http://sites.micro-link.net/zekscrab/

A highly recommended comprehensive study guide to the life and works of William Shakespeare, including play summaries, sonnet analyses and more.

Shakespeare Online

www.shakespeare-online.com

A US site containing free and original information on Shakespeare for students, teachers and Shakespeare enthusiasts.

ShakespeareHelp

www.shakespearehelp.com

A helpful website that offers texts, comments, analysis, message boards and links to related web resources for nine of Shakespeare's best-loved plays.

Teachit

www.teachit.co.uk

An internet library of classroom resources put together by working English teachers. It contains over 4,000 downloadable pages of classroom materials, schemes of work, lesson plans and teaching tools. The website is for ages primary to 16+.

Thesaurus

www.thesaurus.com

On this website you can type in a word and a list of synonyms and antonyms will appear.

Web English Teacher

www.webenglishteacher.com

A teachers' resource site where educators can take advantage of online technology to share ideas and find guidance and inspiration relating to the teaching of English.

Word Detective

www.word-detective.com

A magazine site about words and how to play with them. It is the online version of a popular newspaper column with the same title.

World Book Day

www.worldbookday.com

World Book Day aims to encourage children to explore the pleasures of books and reading. On this website you can find out what this special day is all about.

Worldwide Words

www.worldwidewords.org

A fascinating site for anyone interested in the origins of English words. It is full of English words and phrases, what they mean, where they come from and how they have evolved and been used (or misused). The website is international English, from a British viewpoint.

Young Writer

www.mystworld.com/youngwriter

Young Writer is a magazine which publishes creative writing, prose, poetry, fiction and non-fiction. The material is submitted from around the world by children aged up to 18.

Environment

Environmental organisations have made good use of the internet to raise awareness of sustainable development issues. Whether you want to save the whale or the rainforest, conserve energy resources, recycle household rubbish, check government policy or volunteer for an environmental project, the websites in this section will provide valuable guidance and information.

E 58

A Rocha

Animal Rescuers

ARKive

British Association of Nature
    Conservationists

British Trees

BTCV

Centre for Alternative Technology

Conservation International

Coral Cay Conservation

Department for Environment, Food and
    Rural Affairs

Eco Schools

Ecovolunteer

Endangered Animals of the World

English Nature

Envirolink

Environment Agency

Environmental Investigation Agency

Environmental News Network

Environmental Sites on the Internet

Forestry Commission

Friends of the Earth

Global Witness

Gorilla Foundation

Greenpeace

Grist Magazine

International Fund for Animal Welfare

Learning about Forests

London Wildlife Trust

National Marine Aquarium

Nature Photographers

Naturenet

People and Planet

Polar Bears International

Rainforest Concern

Rainforest Live

Recycle for London

Recycle Now

Royal Society for the Prevention of
    Cruelty to Animals

Royal Society for the Protection of Birds

Save or Delete

Sea Watch Foundation

Shark Trust

Tropical Rainforest Coalition

Waste Watch

Wildfile.co.uk

Woodland Trust

WSPA – World Society for the Protection
    of Animals

WWF – The Conservation Organisation

Yes2Wind

A Rocha

www.arocha.org

A Christian nature conservation organisation, A Rocha projects are community based with an emphasis on practical conservation, environmental education, science and research.

Animal Rescuers

www.animalrescuers.co.uk

A website providing very comprehensive listings of centres, leagues, associations who are all dedicated to preserving, supporting and helping injured and distressed animals.

ARKive

www.arkive.org

ARKive is a centralised digital library of films, photographs and associated recordings of endangered species. This incredible wildlife resource has been created to assist in the conservation and preservation of the well-being of the natural world.

British Association of Nature Conservationists

www.banc.org.uk

The website of the 'think tank' that analyses current issues, future trends and opportunities in the field of conservation.

British Trees

www.british-trees.com

This website provides comprehensive information about native British trees.

BTCV

www.btcv.org

A nationwide organisation that co-ordinates environmental projects and the volunteers required to do the work. You can give as much or as little time as you can spare.

Centre for Alternative Technology

www.cat.org.uk

This environmental charity aims to 'inspire, inform and enable people to live more sustainably'. Offering practical solutions to environmental problems, the centre works in areas such as renewable energy, energy

E59

E 60

efficiency, environmental building and organic growing.

Conservation International

www.conservation.org

Working in over 30 countries, CI's mission is to 'conserve the Earth's natural living heritage, our global biodiversity, and to demonstrate that human societies are able to live harmoniously with nature'. CI's colourful website gives full details of their work.

Coral Cay Conservation

www.coralcay.org

The website of the not-for-profit ecotourism organisation that sends teams of volunteers to survey some of the world's most endangered coral reefs and tropical forests.

Department for Environment, Food and Rural Affairs

www.defra.gov.uk

DEFRA is responsible for the Government's policies and programmes relating to the environment, food and rural affairs. Their website gives a great insight into the depth and breadth of their work.

Eco Schools

www.eco-schools.org

Eco Schools helps to improve the environment of schools, and increase awareness of local environmental issues, through a programme of environmental management and sustainable development education.

Ecovolunteer

www.ecovolunteer.org

Volunteer on this website to take part in environmental conservation programmes. Their projects take place around the world.

Endangered Animals of the World

www.tenan.vuurwerk.nl

An ongoing project that allows students from all over the world a chance to help foster knowledge and appreciation for the plight of the many thousands of endangered animals of the Earth.

English Nature

www.englishnature.org.uk

The work of English Nature the government-funded organisation whose remit is to promote the conservation of England's wildlife and natural features.

Envirolink

www.envirolink.org

A massive site that unites hundreds of organisations and volunteers into an 'online environmental community'. EnviroLink provides comprehensive information and has extensive listings of environmental organisations worldwide. An excellent educational resource.

Environment Agency

www.environment-agency.gov.uk

The leading public agency responsible for protecting and improving the environment in England and Wales. Their website has details of the agency's policy, work, publications and events.

Environmental Investigation Agency

www.eia-international.org

This website contains the fascinating work of the Environmental Investigation Agency, the international campaigning organisation that is committed to investigating and exposing environmental crimes.

Environmental News Network

www.enn.com

An online environmental magazine with an impressive collection of features and the latest environmental news from around the world.

Environmental Sites on the Internet

www.ima.kth.se/im/envsite/envsite.htm

A comprehensive directory of environmental sites. The topics range from acid rain and activism to waste water and whaling.

Forestry Commission

www.forestry.gov.uk

The Forestry Commission, through its Forest Enterprise agencies, manages more than 1,000,000 hectares of land throughout UK and its research programme promotes high standards of sustainable forest management. You can find out what is going on in your local woods through the website's links to habitats, mammals, birds and places to go.

Friends of the Earth

www.foe.co.uk

FoE is the largest international network of environmental groups in the world and is represented in 68 countries. It commissions research and provides information and educational material on environmental issues.

Global Witness

www.globalwitness.org

The website of the hard-hitting, non-govermental investigative organisation that works to expose links between the exploitation of natural resources and human rights abuses around the world.

Gorilla Foundation

www.gorilla.org

Established in 1976, the Gorilla Foundation promotes the protection, preservation and propagation of gorillas.

Greenpeace

www.greenpeace.org

The attractive (green!) website of the high-profile campaigning organisation that uses non-violent, 'creative confrontation' as a means to draw attention to global environmental problems.

Grist Magazine

www.gristmagazine.com

The US-based online environmental magazine that 'tackles environmental topics with irreverence, intelligence and a fresh perspective'. Grist is informative and entertaining, proving that environmentalists CAN have a sense of humour.

International Fund for Animal Welfare

www.ifaw.org

The IFAW is dedicated to the preservation of wildlife in its natural habitat. The website contains stories and reports from across the globe.

Learning about Forests

www.leaf-international.org

The Learning about Forests programme encourages schools to use forests for educational activities. An international internet-based network where schools can share ideas and experiences.

London Wildlife Trust

www.wildlondon.org.uk

The London Wildlife Trust fights to sustain and enhance the capital's natural heritage to create a city richer in wildlife. Nature Reserves, conservation, wildlife facts, childrens club, biological recordings, bees, gardening and much more. If you're interested in wildlife you could join Wildlife Watch, the action club for young environmentalists aged 8–14.

National Marine Aquarium

www.national-aquarium.co.uk

The UK's foremost aquarium, established for the purpose of education, conservation and research. It is a charity dedicated to raising awareness of the oceans.

Nature Photographers

www.naturephotographers.net

An online magazine dedicated to nature photography, with some wonderful pictures and advice for budding photographers.

Naturenet

www.naturenet.net

An appealing site that provides an extensive resource for practical nature conservation and countryside management. It includes issues such as environmental news, laws of the countryside, nature reserves and much more. It is a excellent site for young people interested in nature issues.

People and Planet

www.peopleandplanet.net

This is a top quality website that looks in-depth at the issues of population, poverty, health, consumption and the environment. For each of the 16 topics covered you will find well-written features plus an overview, newsfile, details of books and films, a factfile, features and a glossary.

Polar Bears International

www.polarbearsalive.org

Polar Bears International is dedicated to the conservation of the polar bear. On this website you can explore the latest information and research about one of the most endearing animals in our world and see some wonderful photographs.

Rainforest Concern

www.rainforestconcern.org

This organisation is dedicated to protecting the world's rainforests, the biodiversity they contain and the people who depend on them. You can check their website to see how you can help and they have a special kids section too.

Rainforest Live

www.rainforestlive.org.uk

The attractive, educational website from Paignton Zoo about rainforests. It has excellent material for teachers and kids.

Recycle for London

www.recycleforlondon.com

A helpful website that shows Londoners how they can recycle more of their household waste but the tips and advice are not just for those living in London.

Recycle Now

www.recyclenow.com

Leading UK retailers, local councils and the media have joined together to produce this very attractive, user-friendly site that gives the low-down on the problem of household rubbish and suggests some quick and easy solutions.

Royal Society for the Prevention of Cruelty to Animals

www.rspca.org

This website contains information about the work of the RSPCA and how you can help. Founded in 1824, the Society has worked tirelessly to promote kindness and prevent cruelty to animals. There is a special section on the website for children.

Royal Society for the Protection of Birds

www.rspb.org

The RSPB is the UK charity working to secure a healthy environment for birds and wildlife.

Save or Delete

www.saveordelete.com

Save or Delete campaigns to protect the world's ancient forests and is run by Greenpeace UK.

Sea Watch Foundation

www.seawatchfoundation.org.uk

Sea Watch provides a comprehensive system of surveying and monitoring marine mammals which is crucial to their survival. Learn more from this website about cetaceans (whales, dolphins and porpoises) and find out about sightings around the UK.

Shark Trust

www.sharktrust.org

This UK organisation was set up in 1997 to promote the study, management and conservation of sharks, skates and rays in the UK and internationally.

Tropical Rainforest Coalition

www.rainforest.org

The TRC is a non-profit, volunteer organisation whose mission is to preserve tropical rainforest eco-systems through volunteer action, community education and technical and financial support.

Waste Watch

www.wastewatch.org.uk

You can learn from this website how to recycle almost anything including cans, batteries, fluorescent tubes, bottles and paper. The site has a 'recyclezone' with great education projects and guidance for schools.

Wildfile.co.uk

www.mylinkspage.com/wildfile

This website has extensive links to wildlife trusts around the UK and to other nature and environment sites.

Woodland Trust

www.woodland-trust.org.uk

This website details the work and aims of this major UK conservation charity dedicated to the protection of the country's native woodland heritage.

WSPA – World Society for the Protection of Animals

www.wspa.org.uk

WSPA, the World Society for the Protection of Animals, works with more than 460 member organisations to raise the standard of animal welfare throughout the world.

WWF – The Conservation Organisation

www.panda.org

The website of the global organisation, founded in 1961 and initially known as the World Wildlife Fund, that works to conserve nature through a combination of action, national and international advocacy and campaigning.

Yes2Wind

www.yes2wind.com

A website promoting the use of wind power and raising awareness of its benefits.

Film, Television and Radio

Media institutions are well represented on the internet, with most of them making good use of the latest web technology to promote programmes and films or to stream live radio programmes. In addition to these, you can find websites in this category to help you pursue a career in the industry, (whether in front of or behind the camera), information on taking your first steps as a radio reporter, research to support Media Studies, as well as sites giving you all the glitz and glamour of the Oscars and other awards. **See also related sites in the Drama and Theatre and Media categories.**

Media Institutions and Schools

Academic Info – Film and Television Studies Gateway

BBC Research Central

British Academy of Film and Television Arts

Broadcast Journalism Training Council

Ethnic Multicultural Media Awards

London Film School

MediaEd

National Film and Television School

World Entertainment News Network

Television

Advertising Archives

Artsworld

BBC

British Television Advertising Awards

Broadcast Now

Channel 4

ITN Archive

Royal Television Society

Film

Aardman

BBC Films

BFI National Library

BritMovie

British Film Institute

British Pathe

Cinemas Online

Edinburgh International Film Festival

Empire Online

Film, Art and Creative Technology

First Film Foundation

Golden Globes

Guardian Unlimited – film

Hollywood Reporter

Oscar Awards

Screen Daily

Tookey's Film Guide

Variety

Radio

BBC Digital Radio

BBC Radio

Oneword Radio

Radio Locator

F 66

Media Institutions and Schools

Academic Info – Film and Television Studies Gateway

www.academicinfo.net/film.html

An extensive US directory of online resources for film and television.

BBC Research Central

www.bbcresearchcentral.com

BBC Research Central has over 550,000 document files, 120,000 books, 26 million press cuttings, BBC Television archives from the first day of broadcasting to the current day, sound archives going back to the 1880s and over 4 million photographic images. Is this enough to be getting on with?

British Academy of Film and Television Arts

www.bafta.org

The UK's leading organisation for promoting and rewarding the best of British television, film and interactive media.

Broadcast Journalism Training Council

www.bjtc.org.uk

The BJTC offers essential advice and guidance about the skills and knowledge you will need if you are considering a career in journalism on television, radio or online.

Ethnic Multicultural Media Awards

www.emma.tv

The Ethnic Multicultural Media Awards were set up to celebrate multicultural achievement in the media and stand 'as an important statement for Britain's ethnically varied society'.

London Film School

www.lifs.org.uk

The first step into the filmmaking industry. All of the information about the school is here on this website, including details of courses on offer.

MediaEd

www.mediaed.org.uk

Funded by the BFI, this is an excellent resource site for teachers, students and anyone else interested in media and moving image education at primary and secondary levels.

National Film and Television School

www.nftsfilm-tv.ac.uk

NFTS is a leading centre for professional training in film, television and related media industries. It offers both full-time and a wide range of short courses.

World Entertainment News Network

www.wenn.com

WENN delivers up-to-the-minute entertainment news and photos to the world's media.

Television

Advertising Archives

www.advertisingarchives.co.uk

Advertising Archives has probably the largest collection of adverts in the world and some dating back 150 years. A unique reference resource for enthusiasts and collectors or those looking for an insight into social history.

Artsworld

www.artsworld.com

This website contains listings, reviews and programmes for the Sky digital television channel dedicated to the arts.

BBC

www.bbc.co.uk

The home page for the huge family of great BBC websites, which total more than two million pages. The easy-to-follow directory helps you find just what you are looking for.

British Television Advertising Awards

www.btaa.co.uk

The British Television Advertising Awards recognise and reward the best television and cinema commercials of the year. They are available to view online.

Broadcast Now

www.broadcastnow.co.uk

The online newspaper about the UK television and radio industry.

Channel 4

www.channel4.com

This website offers much more than television listings. It has news, sport, health, history, games, competitions and many interactive elements too.

ITN Archive

www.itnarchive.com

The ITN's huge archive resource covering news, sport, drama, documentaries, features and oodles more.

Royal Television Society

www.rts.org.uk

The RTS provides a forum for discussion and debate on all aspects of the television industry. They also manage a series of award schemes, including for student television.

Film

Aardman

www.aardman.com

The home of Wallace and Gromit and the chickens from Chicken Run. A great site with project news plus a history of the Aardman team and the possibility of a virtual tour around the studio.

BBC Films

www.bbc.co.uk/films

The BBC's excellent guide to films. The website includes movie news, reviews, previews and discussions and covers both the BBC's film programming and the latest cinema releases.

BFI National Library

**www.bfi.org.uk/nationallibrary/
index.html**

The BFI National Library provides access to a large collection of documentation and information on film and television. Their website shows how their services can be accessed.

BritMovie

www.britmovie.co.uk

Dedicated to British cinema, BritMovie holds extensive information including A to Z film listings, biographies of British directors and actors, details of film studios and much more. This is a great site for British film fans.

British Film Institute

www.bfi.org.uk

A website all about the work of the BFI, which has been promoting greater understanding and appreciation of film and television culture since it was established in 1933. Its 'Sight and Sound' magazine includes reviews and features and it also has links to www.bft.org.uk/nationallibrary/indes.html which provides access to a large collection of documentation and information on film and television.

British Pathe

www.britishpathe.com

Previews of Pathe newsreels, with more than 3,500 hours of film archives covering news, sport, social history and entertainment from 1896 to 1970 are available on this website.

Cinemas Online

www.cinemas-online.co.uk

An excellent 'what's on' film site that includes gossip, features, competitions and forums.

Edinburgh International Film Festival

www.edfilmfest.org.uk

An attractive and entertaining website about the world-famous Edinburgh International Film Festival.

Empire Online

www.empireonline.co.uk

An entertaining, extensive and informative website from the UK's leading film magazine.

Film, Art and Creative Technology

www.fact.co.uk

The website about the work of FACT, which claims to be 'the UK's leading organisation for the support and exhibition of film, video and new media projects'.

First Film Foundation

www.firstfilm.co.uk

The First Film Foundation provides support, advice and information to help new writers, producers and directors to make their first feature film.

Golden Globes

www.thegoldenglobes.com

The Golden Globe awards, which honour achievements in film and television, are given by the Hollywood Foreign Press Association in the USA.

Guardian Unlimited – film

http://film.guardian.co.uk

An intelligent look at films plus news, reviews, features and interviews.

Hollywood Reporter

www.thehollywoodreporter.com

The website of Hollywood's entertainment industry magazine. It covers television, music and new media as well as films.

Oscar Awards

www.oscars.com

The official Oscars' site, full of glitz and glamour.

Screen Daily

www.screendaily.com

A daily news service for the global film industry with links to reviews, festivals, magazines, listings, box office statistics and much more.

Tookey's Film Guide

www.tookeysfilmguide.com

This website contains not just reviews of the latest films. Tookey's Film Guide also covers every significant film since 1902 and it is possibly the largest collection of film reviews online. The Film Guide is compiled and maintained by well-known film critic, Chris Tookey.

Variety

www.variety.com

An entertaining site from the long-running and popular showbiz magazine.

Radio

BBC Digital Radio

www.bbc.co.uk/digitalradio

A website all about digital radio, from the BBC – what it is, how it works and how to listen to it.

BBC Radio

www.bbc.co.uk/radio

Your gateway to all the BBC's international, national, regional and local stations. You can take your pick of your station by genre too.

Oneword Radio

www.oneword.co.uk

The website of the world's first radio station featuring plays, books, comedy and discussion.

Radio Locator

www.radio-locator.com

Radio Locator claims to be the most comprehensive radio station search engine on the internet. They have links to over 10,000 radio station web pages and over 2,500 audio streams from around the world.

F70

Geography

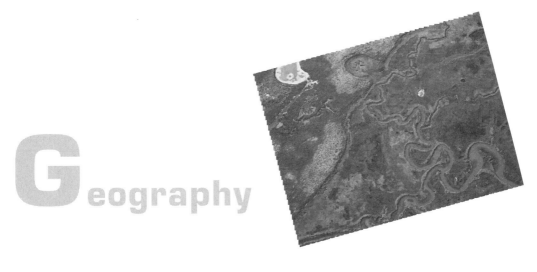

Geography students and teachers will find sites here containing a huge range of resources, courses and lessons covering topics within the National Curriculum. A wide range of websites with reference material, statistical information and country profiles are also featured. **See also the Science category.**

Atlapedia Online

Aurora Page

British Antarctic Survey

Calendar Zone

CountryReports

Coursework

Cultural Survival

Earth Observatory

Earthquakes

Essential Guide to Rocks

Field Studies Council

Geographical Association

Geography High

Geography in Action

Geography Site

GeographyIQ

Geographypages

GeoInteractive – Geography Resources

GeoResources

Global Eye

Global Warming

IB Geography

Internet Geographer

Internet Geography

Kay's AS and A2 Geography

Met Office

National Geographic

Ordnance Survey

Pupil Vision

Rainforest Alliance

Revisiontime

Royal Geographical Society

S-Cool

Standard Grade Geography

UpMyStreet

Volcano World

World Atlas

World Factbook

Atlapedia Online

www.atlapedia.com

A US site aimed at school students with physical and political maps plus key facts and statistics on countries of the world.

Aurora Page

www.geo.mtu.edu/weather/aurora

What is the Aurora Borealis? What causes it? This website provides information, links and images about the "Northern Lights".

British Antarctic Survey

www.antarctica.ac.uk

A website all about the work of the British Antarctic Survey, which has carried out scientific research on and around Antarctica for almost 60 years.

Calendar Zone

www.calendarzone.com

The Calendar Zone contains celestial, cultural and religious calendars. There are all sorts of calendars here on this American website.

CountryReports

www.countryreports.org

CountryReports have profiles of over 260 countries. You will find basic geographic and economic data on this website plus the latest news from the country concerned. It is a useful reference tool for geography students.

Coursework

www.coursework.info

Coursework claims to offer the largest database of UK orientated coursework in the world. It is a useful learning resource and the material is suitable for GCSE, AS/A Level and IB students.

Cultural Survival

www.cs.org

A website that promotes 'the rights, voices and visions of indigenous peoples'. It has useful information for anyone studying population and migration issues.

Earth Observatory

www.earthobservatory.nasa.gov

The earth's climate and environmental change are the key areas of work for NASA's Earth Observatory. A website where the public can obtain satellite imagery and scientific information about our planet.

Earthquakes

www.earthquakes.bgs.ac.uk

The British Geological Survey has put together this comprehensive site where you can learn all about earthquakes.

Essential Guide to Rocks

www.bbc.co.uk/education/rocks

The BBC's online guide to British rocks. You can take virtual walks around Britain discovering the rocks of our urban landscape, take a look at Britain's rocky past or conduct field trips and experiments on rocks in and around your home.

Field Studies Council

www.field-studies-council.org

The FSC is a pioneering educational charity committed to bringing environmental understanding to all. The outdoor classroom area has activities for eco-adventures for schools plus Key Stage3 science/biology, Key Stage3 geography, 16+ biology information and much more.

Geographical Association

www.geography.org.uk

The Geographical Association's mission is to further the teaching of geography and to communicate the value of learning geography. The association has over 10,000 members including teachers, academic geographers, educators and trainers.

Geography High

www.geographyhigh.connectfree. co.uk

A virtual reality school with only geography on the curriculum. Amongst the 'classrooms' you will find a weather forecast room, geology department, map room and special areas for pupils at all levels of study, each covering a wide variety of curriculum-related subjects.

Geography in Action

www.geographyinaction.co.uk

Geography resources for all students and teachers, but with emphasis on the Northern Ireland curriculum.

Geography Site

www.geography-site.co.uk

The Geography Site is committed to providing students and teachers with high quality, original, reliable resources for learning and teaching geography. It is aimed mainly at the 12 to 16 age group but some resources are suitable for older students.

GeographyIQ

www.geographyiq.com

Geography IQ's world map is packed with geographic, economic, political, historical and cultural information about every country in the world.

Geographypages

www.geographypages.co.uk

An up to date geography resource site supported by the Royal Geographical Society and the Institute of British Geographers. It covers Key Stages 1 to 3, GCSE and AS/A levels.

GeoInteractive – Geography Resources

www.geointeractive.co.uk

A new website launched in 2004 with geography resources for teachers, featuring contribution and subscription sections plus the facility to use e-learning credits here.

GeoResources

www.georesources.co.uk

A website that is packed full of geography links divided into Key Stage3, GCSE and AS/A level and covering all national curriculum topics. You can also try doing some virtual fieldwork, check out the case

G73

studies section, make use of the online maps or peek at the photo gallery.

Global Eye

www.globaleye.org.uk

An online resource based on the Global Eye, the magazine for schools promoting understanding of global development issues.

Global Warming

www.epa.gov/globalwarming

This site from the US Environmental Protection Agency, provides extensive information about climate change and global warming. It has an excellent young persons' zone too.

IB Geography

www.ibgeog.com

This site from the International School of Toulouse is designed specifically for IB students and teachers of geography and contains extensive resource material.

Internet Geographer

www.internetgeographer.co.uk

A directory of useful geography-related websites which are grouped according to subject with brief descriptions and ratings.

Internet Geography

www.geography.learnontheinternet. co.uk

A great website packed with resources for teachers and Key Stage3 and GCSE students with material on environmental, physical, human and economic geography covering every part of the curriculum.

Kay's AS and A2 Geography

www.geography.btinternet.co.uk

This website contains helpful study material for AS/A level and Scottish Higher geography students.

Met Office

www.met-office.gov.uk

It is not just the UK weather on the Meteorological Office website, it also has interesting features, world weather and severe weather warnings.

National Geographic

www.nationalgeographic.com

The website of the National Geographic Society contains extensive (and inspiring) resources, features, photographs and articles. Resources include links to Adventure and Exploration, Animals and Nature, Maps and Geography and various magazines including one specifically for children.

Ordnance Survey

www.ordnancesurvey.co.uk

The official site of the UK's mapping agency, offering a comprehensive range of both paper maps and digital map data files for computers. There are lots of geographical facts and figures about the UK plus a 'free and fun' area.

Pupil Vision

www.pupilvision.com

An attractive, multi-award winning website with extensive resources for GCSE and AS/A level students.

Rainforest Alliance

www.rainforest-alliance.org

This international conservation organisation aims to protect ecosystems and improve biodiversity conservation through encouraging companies and landowners to meet rigorous standards for protecting the environment. The site has a special teachers and children section with information and activities.

Revisiontime

www.revisiontime.com

A portal site with links to useful geography websites that are suitable for both GCSE and A level students.

Royal Geographical Society

www.rgs.org

An inspiring website about the Royal Geographical Society, which since 1830 has been supporting research, education and training in geography and promoting the wider public understanding and enjoyment of this popular subject.

S-Cool

www.s-cool.co.uk

On this website you just click GCSE or A Level and AS Level and once you have selected geography you can choose the topics that you want to study which cover all areas of the curriculum.

Standard Grade Geography

www.scalloway.org.uk

An online interactive resource for standard grade geography students in Scotland, but useful for GCSE students too.

UpMyStreet

www.upmystreet.co.uk

On this website you can type in your postcode and receive a wealth of local information about the area where you live.

Volcano World

http://volcano.und.nodak.edu

Learn about volcanoes around the world on this site, which claims to be 'the web's premier source of volcano information'.

World Atlas

www.worldatlas.com

A website containing maps, facts, figures, flags and much more. It covers every country in the world and you can carry out a variety of searches too.

World Factbook

www.odci.gov/cia/publications/fact book/index.html

A very useful site hosted by the CIA full of facts about the countries of the world. It is updated weekly.

History

Choose from a wide range of websites covering history topics, including those required for the National Curriculum. These fascinating sites cover every era from ancient history through to World War 2, plus subjects such as the British Monarchy, biographies of historical figures, archaeology and genealogy, history links around the world, as well as numerous other learning and reference resources. **See also the Politics category.**

Active History

Battle of Hastings 1066

BBC History

BBC People's War

Black Presence in Britain

British History

British History Online

British Monarchy

Burnt Cakes

Current Archaeology

Diary of Samuel Pepys

DocumentsOnline

Early British History

European History

Eye Witness to History

Family Records

From Dot to Domesday

GCSE History Pages

Genes Reunited

Great War 1914–1918

Historical Association

History Channel

History Learning Site

History Mad

History on the Net

History Today

History World

HistoryNet

Historysite

Learn History

Learning Curve

National Archives

Old Maps

Prehistoric Planet

Regia Anglorum

Revolutionary Players

Rulers

SchoolHistory

Spartacus Educational

ThinkHistory

This Day in History

Tudor History

Tudor Menu

Union Makes Us Strong

Union of the Crowns

Vietnam Veterans Memorial Fund

Western Culture

Women's Library

World at War 1939–1945

World of Royalty

World War I: Trenches on the Web

WorldWar2

Active History

www.activehistory.co.uk

An award-winning website from Wolverhampton Grammar School's History Department. Developed by a classroom teacher and his students for other teachers and students, Active History is suitable for ages 11 to 18 and includes virtual interviews with historical figures, decision-making games, sourcework exercises, interactive quizzes and in-depth investigations.

Battle of Hastings 1066

www.battle1066.com

With its bright, modern graphics, this site covers far more than its name suggests. The topics include not only the Normans, the background to the battle and its consequences, but also the Romans, Vikings and Saxons.

BBC History

www.bbc.co.uk/history

This is another winning BBC site with in-depth articles on a range of topics (from Ancient History to World War Two), history forums and chats, a great multimedia zone, a history reading room and much more.

BBC People's War

www.bbc.co.uk/dna/ww2

This engaging BBC website records personal and family experiences of the Second World War, from ordinary people who found themselves living through extraordinary times. There are accounts from people who lived and worked at home as well as those who fought abroad.

Black Presence in Britain

www.blackpresence.co.uk

This website covers Black British history, from the slave trade through to the first black people in Britain and the current day. There are many black Britons listed, some famous and some just ordinary citizens. All of them contribute to Britain's fascinating hidden history.

British History

www.britannia.com/history

Britannia's British History claims to be 'the internet's most comprehensive treatment of the times, places, events and people of British history'. It contains narrative histories, timelines, biographies, glossaries and lots more. It is an extensive resource for students and teachers.

British History Online

www.british-history.ac.uk

From the Institute of Historical Research and the History of Parliament Trust, this digital library of British historical sources will be of interest to historians, teachers and students.

British Monarchy

www.royal.gov.uk

The official website of the British Monarchy includes information about the work of the monarchy today, background on the Royal Family, the history of the monarchy and an insight into royal residences and artworks.

Burnt Cakes

www.burntcakes.com

Burnt Cakes is 'dedicated to better history teaching and learning'. There is plenty on this website to interest history students, as well as top class teaching resources, some of which are free.

Current Archaeology

www.archaeology.co.uk

The online version of Current Archaeology magazine. Aimed at ordinary archaeological enthusiasts, this is a great site for anyone interested in what is happening in the world of archaeology.

Diary of Samuel Pepys

www.pepysdiary.com

A fascinating interactive diary of Samuel Pepys' descriptions of everyday life in Seventeenth Century London.

DocumentsOnline

www.documentsonline.pro.gov.uk

DocumentsOnline provides online access to the National Archives' collection of digitised public records, including academic and genealogical sources.

Early British History

www.webmesh.co.uk/britishprehistory.htm

A website presenting Britain's history before the Romans. A site built by a history enthusiast who has managed to put together an excellent collection of relevant documents.

European History

www.europeanhistory.about.com

A guide to European history pointing to interesting history sites and packed with well documented stories.

Eye Witness to History

www.eyewitnesstohistory.com

This website provides history through the eyes of those who lived it, from the ancient world to the twenty-first century. It includes special sections on the two World Wars.

Family Records

www.familyrecords.gov.uk

This government site is perfect for family history researchers, helping them find their way around various records.

From Dot to Domesday

www.stephen.j.murray.btinternet.co.uk

How far back in time do you want to go? Here on this website you will find Britain's history from its creation at the end of the ice age to the time of the Domesday Book.

GCSE History Pages

www.historygcse.org

This website provides useful free online help for GCSE history students, written by an experienced teacher and examiner.

Genes Reunited

www.genesreunited.co.uk

From the creators of Friends Reunited, Genes Reunited allows you to build your family tree and create a record of your family history. And when adding your details, you will help create one of the largest genealogy databases in the UK.

Great War 1914–1918

www.greatwar.co.uk

A well researched reference work on the First World War, that brings events to life. Written by two expert historians with over 30 years experience of visiting and studying the battlefields of the Western Front.

Historical Association

www.history.org.uk

As well as information about the work of the association, this site points to useful links and articles from popular history magazines and suggests activities involving history research.

History Channel

www.thehistorychannel.com

An information-packed website from television's History Channel. You can search by title, date or subject. It is a great resource for exam and revision help too.

History Learning Site

www.historylearningsite.co.uk

Key Stage 3, GCSE or advanced level history courses are covered here on this website. You just click on the topics and sub-topics listed for detailed and informative articles.

History Mad

www.historymad.com

A portal site, created and maintained by the head of history at a school in Hull. It has links to recommended history sites, which are all vetted for suitability for secondary level students.

History on the Net

www.historyonthenet.com

A well organised website that provides historical information, linked to the national curriculum, for teachers and students. In addition to the site's resources you will find a range of interactive activities with a history theme.

H80

History Today

www.historytoday.com

Articles from History Today magazine published since 1980 are available here. There is also an extensive section with resources for GCSE and A level history students.

History World

www.historyworld.net

Part of the National Grid for Learning, this site is an extensive history resource for teachers and students. At its core are 400 interconnecting narratives and 6,000 selected events.

HistoryNet

www.thehistorynet.com

At HistoryNet you can find good written articles focusing on the humanity of history in this growing historical archive. A history lover's place whether you are a novice, student or expert.

Historysite

www.thehistorysite.co.uk

An easy-to-use interactive history lesson site for years 7 to 11. It is maintained by an experienced teacher and a team of student authors.

Learn History

www.learnhistory.org.uk

A website providing free history resources for students, covering all the national curriculum topics, including PowerPoint lessons, quizzes and research help.

Learning Curve

www.learningcurve.pro.gov.uk

From the National Archives, Learning Curve is an online teaching resource structured to tie in with the history national curriculum for key stages 2–5. It contains a varied range of original sources including documents, photographs, films and sound recordings.

National Archives

www.nationalarchives.gov.uk

The National Archives brings together the sites of the former Public Record Office and Historical Manuscripts Commission. It is a national resource for anyone interested in documents relating to British history.

Old Maps

www.old-maps.co.uk

Type in your town and this site will show you a map of what your neighbourhood was like during the second half of the nineteenth century.

Prehistoric Planet

www.prehistoricplanet.com

An internet magazine dedicated to the prehistoric age. In addition to interesting articles and features, there is a dinosaurs section, fossil news and cool prehistoric links.

Regia Anglorum

www.regia.org

Fancy living like a Norman lord, or an Anglo-Saxon peasant? Regia Anglorum is a re-enactment society that recreates the lives (and deaths) of Anglo-Saxons, Normans and Vikings.

Revolutionary Players

www.revolutionaryplayers.org.uk

Supported by the New Opportunities Fund, this project focuses on the history of the Industrial Revolution in the West Midlands in Britain between 1700 and 1830. It uses images from museums, archives and libraries to depict the history of the period.

Rulers

www.rulers.org

A directory of the heads of state and heads of government of every country and territory in the world, dating back to the 1700s.

SchoolHistory

www.schoolhistory.co.uk

A top history site with online lessons and comprehensive links to internet material for history students from primary to A level. Over 1,000 reviewed historical sites are listed and you will also find interactive games and quizzes, freely downloadable resources and online revision material.

Spartacus Educational

www.spartacus.schoolnet.co.uk

Spartacus Educational is an online series of history encyclopedias. A massive resource for students and teachers, the well set out directory contains material on a huge range of topics, each with a narrative, illustrations and primary sources plus links to related material.

ThinkHistory

www.thinkhistory.co.uk

A teacher-designed website allowing Key Stage 3 and GCSE history students and their teachers to access homework and revision resources.

This Day in History

www.thisdayinhistory.com

From this website you can find out what happened on any given date in the past. The features are updated by the History Channel.

Tudor History

www.tudorhistory.org

The perfect site for anyone studying Tudor History or if you are just interested in this period in history. It is a great site full of entertaining and humorous stories as well as useful resource material.

Tudor Menu

www.tudors.crispen.org

An inspirational website for anyone studying the Tudor period with material covering a range of topics such as the six wives of Henry VIII, family trees, music, arts, heraldry and a fascinating account of the life of women in Tudor England.

Union Makes Us Strong

www.unionhistory.info

A site that highlights the role of the trade unions in developing Britain's history and economy.

Union of the Crowns

www.unionofthecrowns.com

An interesting, attractive, illustrated and educational site about how the English and Scottish crowns were united in 1603.

Vietnam Veterans Memorial Fund

www.teachvietnam.org

In addition to preserving the legacy of the Vietnam Veterans Memorial, the VVMF serves to educate young and old about the Vietnam War and its lasting impact.

Western Culture

www.westernculture.com

This website is essentially a collection of links to sites about western culture, from the ancient Middle East to late twentieth century. The site also contains sections on Christianity, Judaism and Islam.

Women's Library

www.thewomenslibrary.ac.uk

This cultural centre hosts the most extensive collection dedicated to women's history in the UK. Although the online information is not very comprehensive, it is a great place to visit and the site provides details about current events and exhibitions.

World at War 1939–1945

www.worldwar2history.net

A detailed and well-illustrated day-by-day history of the war with links to related sites.

World of Royalty

www.royalty.nu

This website contains anything and everything about royalty from around the world. As well as modern royalty and both ancient and more recent history, there are sections on royal genealogy, royal mysteries and romances, royal myths and legends and even royal films.

World War I: Trenches on the Web

www.worldwar1.com

An internet history of the Great War with articles, pictures and other exhibits about the experiences of the soldiers who fought in the trenches of the Western Front during the First World War.

WorldWar2

www.worldwar-2.net

Day-by-day timelines of every event during World War 2 covering the war in Europe, the Holocaust, the war at sea, the war in the desert. It includes Asia and the Pacific and the Americas.

Information Technology

This category includes information from how to organise your data in neat databases through to how to build your own website. It also contains GCSE and A Level resources, how to establish local school networks, guides for schools on purchasing ICT products and the latest news, resources and trends in IT for teachers, pupils and parents.

321Clipart

Apple

Barry's Clipart Server

British Educational Communications and
   Technology Agency

CNET Help

CompInfo

Computing Students

Create Your Own Webpage

D and T online

Design and Tech

Design Technology Department

Dummies

Education Community

Free Images

Freeskills

Gibson Research Corporation

ICT Advice

ICT GCSE

ICT Register

ICTforALL

Independent ICT Procurement Advisory
   Service

Interactive Essentials

Internet 101

IT Reviews

Learn the Net

Learning HTML for Kids

MacInTouch

MailWasher

MaxPC

Microsoft Kids

Netdictionary

NetLingo

PC Advisor

PC Pitstop

PC TechGuide

PCMechanic

REM

Scanning Basics

School Resources

Symantec Security Check

Teach ICT

ThinkQuest

Webopedia

Wired News

321Clipart

www.321clipart.com

A collection of clipart and graphics to help webmasters design and add colour to their sites. The graphics can be used for DTP projects too.

Apple

www.apple.com

Apple's products are in constant competition with IT's market leader, Microsoft. Apple's official site promotes their latest technologies in multimedia products and applications.

Barry's Clipart Server

www.barrysclipart.com

This website contains clipart, animations and fonts by the thousand plus links to more clipart and pictures. It is useful for website design or any other personal non-profit DTP project.

British Educational Communications and Technology Agency

www.becta.org.uk

A website that details the work of BECTA, the government's key partner in the development and delivery of its ICT and e-learning strategy for schools.

CNET Help

www.help.com

This website provides online courses (some free), CD tutorials, tech forums, newsletters and lots more for IT buffs who want to keep up to date with the latest issues.

CompInfo

www.compinfo.co.uk

An extensive directory of sites relating to the IT industry, covering computer news, magazines, books, events and much more.

Computing Students

www.computingstudents.com

Learn the basics of computing and ICT on this website. While designed for AS/A-level students, this site offers information and resources suitable for all levels.

Create Your Own Webpage

www.smplanet.com/webpage/webpage.html

A simple step-by-step guide to creating your own web pages that is aimed at young students.

D and T online

www.dtonline.org

This site supports the national curriculum and provides free access to a wide range of design and technology materials, resources and software. It is suitable mainly for key stages 3 and 4.

Design and Tech

www.designandtech.com

An attractive website that aims to provide a comprehensive, easy-to-use index of information relating to design and technology at each key stage. You can also submit your work and your school's D and T site.

Design Technology Department

www.design-technology.org

Created to provide free educational materials for schools and colleges, Design Technology Department is an excellent resource covering a huge range of subjects for all of the key stages.

Dummies

www.dummies.com

Dummies books, features and articles to make 'less of a dummie' out of their readers with step by step series of internet and information technology reading tutorials.

Education Community

www.theeducationcommunity. com

The Education Community is a free collaboration service to support school managers and teachers in the effective use of ICT. The home page contains an overview of the latest content and resources that you will find throughout the site.

Free Images

www.freeimages.co.uk

This website provides free images, design tips and presentation templates to make your website and DTP projects easier.

Freeskills

www.freeskills.com

Freeskills produce over 450 free online tutorials, from entry level word processing to advanced techniques covering areas such as web development and network routing.

Gibson Research Corporation

www.grc.com

IT projects, security software updates, research features and advice are all available on this website from a passionate IT guru.

ICT Advice

www.ictadvice.org.uk

This website provides advice, services and resources for those who manage ICT in schools. It covers teaching, learning, administration, policies, technology, ask an expert and new2computers (especially for first time computer users).

ICT GCSE

www.ictgcse.com

An extremely helpful site for anyone completing ICT projects involving databases, websites, presentations, spreadsheets and word processing.

185

ICT Register

www.ict-register.net

Teachers will find a wide range of services on this website as the ICT Register is designed to promote the sharing between schools of their ICT experiences and expertise.

ICTforALL

www.ictforall.co.uk

ICTforALL provides resources to support work at key stages 3 and 4, help with improving grades, worksheet downloads and ICT links.

Independent ICT Procurement Advisory Service

www.ipas.ngfl.gov.uk

The website of the IPAS provides a guide for schools to the purchase of ICT products and services. It contains heaps of advice, guidance and interactive learning resources to aid decision making.

Interactive Essentials

www.interactiveessentials.co.uk

Interactive Essentials is a company dedicated to producing the highest quality educational software. They specialise in software for whole-class teaching using interactive whiteboards. The software is tailored to the national curriculum, providing teaching resources for use across the primary curriculum and to key stage 3.

Internet 101

www.internet101.org

The internet for beginners and not just children as this site is great for older learners too. It is ideal for anyone who wants to know just the basics and to have fun on the internet without having to learn all the techy bits.

IT Reviews

www.itreviews.co.uk

Unbiased reports on computer hardware, software and games, plus editorials and frequently asked questions are all available from this website.

Learn the Net

www.learnthenet.com

This website provides tutorials, features and articles about what you can achieve while on the internet, combined with links to other interesting sites.

Learning HTML for Kids

www.goodellgroup.com/tutorial/index.html

A step-by-step tutorial to help you learn HTML in 12 easy lessons.

MacInTouch

www.macintouch.com

A website providing detailed news and reviews of Apple Mac technologies and software. It is a good site to keep you up to date with the latest from Apple.

MailWasher

www.mailwasher.net

A free 'spam' fighter that protects your inbox by stopping unwanted emails from reaching your computer.

MaxPC

www.maxpc.co.uk

An online PC magazine with the usual mix of product reviews, gadgets, the latest news and tutorials.

Microsoft Kids

www.microsoft.com/kids

This website is a gateway to www.microsoft.com but with tailored information for kids. It offers product information, security updates, training tutorials as well as the latest news from the IT market's world leader.

Netdictionary

www.netdictionary.com

An extremely useful site that looks into the ever-changing world of the English language in cyberspace. It has an alphabetical guide to the internet's technical, cultural and humorous terms.

NetLingo

www.netlingo.com

At NetLingo you can learn 'netiquette' for use in emails and chat rooms. NetLingo contains an extensive dictionary of internet terms and will help you learn the lingo used in the online world.

PC Advisor

www.pcadvisor.co.uk

From PC Advisor magazine, this site offers comprehensive, impartial and practical advice, information and equipment reviews – in plain English.

PC Pitstop

www.pcpitstop.com

Your PC's performances can be tested here for free. A useful tool for advanced users and novices alike.

PC TechGuide

www.pctechguide.com

A website providing easy to follow guides covering components, storage systems, multimedia, input-output and communications. There are also lots of clear tutorials.

PCMechanic

www.pcmech.com

PC Mechanic aims to provide easy, plain English information on computers and includes tutorials, background information on hardware and explanations about how things work.

REM

www.r-e-m.co.uk

REM provide educational software to help from early learning to secondary and adult education. Specific applications for Apple Mac are also available.

Scanning Basics

www.scantips.com

This website has good advice about scanning techniques and the latest information on scanning software for transforming printed text and photographs into digital files.

School Resources

www.school-resources.co.uk

School Resources provides education information, resources and ICT for teachers and students. It includes computer projects, ICT quizzes and homework help amongst many other features.

Symantec Security Check

www.symantec.com/securitycheck

This website offers free scanning facilities that detect viruses on your computer or check if your PC is at risk from hackers or other online threats. This facility is hosted by Symantec, one of the leaders in virus protection software. Their main site also offers information about the latest viruses, worms or trojans.

Teach ICT

www.teach-ict.com

An attractive and well-structured site for ICT teachers and students. The resources available cover students at Key Stage 3, GCSE and AS/A level.

ThinkQuest

www.thinkquest.org

ThinkQuest has an international website-building competition where teams of students and teachers are challenged to build websites on educational topics.

Webopedia

www.webopedia.com

An online dictionary and search engine for computer and internet terminology. The 'Did You Know' section is particularly interesting.

Wired News

www.wired.com

This website has all the latest cool news from the world of technology.

98

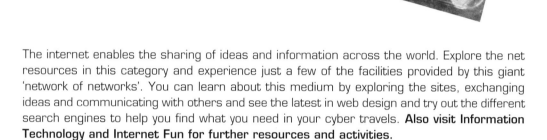

Internet

The internet enables the sharing of ideas and information across the world. Explore the net resources in this category and experience just a few of the facilities provided by this giant 'network of networks'. You can learn about this medium by exploring the sites, exchanging ideas and communicating with others and see the latest in web design and try out the different search engines to help you find what you need in your cyber travels. **Also visit Information Technology and Internet Fun for further resources and activities.**

Alltheweb

AltaVista

Antivirus Software

AOL (UK)

Ask Jeeves

Beegoo

British Information

British Web Design and Marketing
   Association

BT Openworld – Safer Surfing

Computer Active

Computer Crime and Internet-Related
   Crime

Cookie Central

Download.com

EmoticonUniverse

ePals Classroom Exchange

Excite

Firewall Guide

Freeware Arena

Google

Internet News

Internet Watch Foundation

ISP Review

KartOO

Kid Link

Kids Freeware

Kids' Space Connection

KidsCom

Living Internet

LookSmart

Lycos

mail2web

Metacrawler

Mirago

MSN

Net4Nowt

Netiquette

Outlook and Exchange Solutions Center

Photobucket

Plagiarism

Register

SpamCop

Stealth Message

think U know

Wanadoo

WatchThatPage

Web Talk Radio Show

WebMonkey

Webuser Magazine

WindowsSecurity

Working to Halt Online Abuse

Yahoo!

Alltheweb

www.alltheweb.com

Alltheweb claims to allow anyone to find anything faster than with any other search engine.

AltaVista

www.altavista.com

The leading provider of an extensive range of search services.

Antivirus Software

www.software-antivirus.com

At this website you can check out the latest viruses or internet worms along with antivirus software reviews and recommendations. A good initiative from a group of experienced, independent computer experts.

AOL (UK)

www.aol.co.uk

America OnLine is the UK's leading online services provider. To get the best from their service you'll have to become an AOL member.

Ask Jeeves

www.ask.com

The leading provider of world-class information retrieval technologies, brands and services. You can also search for pictures, products and news.

Beegoo

www.beegoo.com

An easy-to-use UK specific search engine.

British Information

www.britishinformation.com

A UK specific internet directory and search engine with a range of features and services.

British Web Design and Marketing Association

www.bwdma.co.uk

The BWDMA aims to improve e-business

standards through sharing knowledge and understanding and the proliferation of best practice. Their website includes interesting articles and features about the internet world.

BT Openworld – Safer Surfing

www.btopenworld.com/safersurfing

This website provides sound guidance from BT to help parents and teachers ensure the internet is safe for children to use. It includes general advice, email protection, PC protection and parental control.

Computer Active

www.computeractive.co.uk

The online version of the leading UK computer magazine. It also covers peripherals, software, the internet, gaming and more.

Computer Crime and Internet-Related Crime

www.met.police.uk/computercrime

This website provides helpful guidance from the Metropolitan Police on how to spot and report computer and internet-related crime.

Cookie Central

www.cookiecentral.com

What are net cookies? Find out here all about this little concept that plays an important part of the whole internet experience.

Download.com

www.download.com

A popular site with lots of software you can download. Apart from freeware and upgrades there is good software on sale

here and you can review and compare prices.

EmoticonUniverse

www.emoticonuniverse.com

A complete directory of emoticons including latest symbols, internet slang and acronyms. Emoticons help to express feelings when writing emails. Visit the website often to keep up to date with the latest or to submit your own.

ePals Classroom Exchange

www.epals.com

This website helps you to get online and chat to 16,000 classrooms in more than 100 countries, speaking 60 languages. A good international project that aims to bring together students from around the world in a safe environment.

Excite

www.excite.co.uk

Excite is more than a search engine. It has a lot of local information, e-cards, an instant translation service, games, travel, horoscope, entertainment and more.

Firewall Guide

www.firewallguide.com

A website providing good independent advice and reviews about firewall software and other security and privacy products available on the market for both home and office use.

Freeware Arena

www.freewarearena.com

Freeware Arena offers hundreds of free, downloadable programmes including games, tools and screensavers. An excellent section with downloadable tutorials.

Google

www.google.co.uk

Recognised as the market-leader of search engines, Google also offers a range of other services and tools including discussion groups, internet images, the latest news and translation services.

Internet News

www.internetnews.com

A US site with the latest news from the internet world and business trends in the IT industry.

Internet Watch Foundation

www.iwf.org.uk

This organisation fights against illegal material on the internet. Internet users in the UK can report here any material which they believe might be illegal.

ISP Review

www.ispreview.co.uk

A website containing news and reviews relating to Internet Service Providers (ISPs) worldwide from a consumer perspective.

KartOO

www.kartoo.com

A visual search engine that displays its results in a diagram showing how relevant sites are related. The graphics are excellent.

Kid Link

www.kidlink.org

Children from around the world can communicate with each other through email or real time chat. Over 160 countries currently participate and the site also offers information for teachers, parents and educational authorities.

Kids Freeware

www.kidsfreeware.com

Kids Freeware offers superb web freeware suitable for kids, from games to interesting web utilities plus school resources and a special area for teachers and parents.

Kids' Space Connection

www.ks-connection.org

Kids' Space was created to foster literacy, artistic expression, and cross-cultural understanding among the world's children.

KidsCom

www.kidscom.co.uk

KidsCom provides safe and free email for children. It is also a good net resource with separate sections containing games, safe message boards and jokes.

Living Internet

www.livinginternet.com

A simple and easy to follow site answering any questions you may have about the internet including its history, design, usage and a lot more. It is a great site for novices and nerds alike.

LookSmart

www.looksmart.com

This search engine is linked to AltaVista and the search results include comments to help users decide on the most relevant results that match requests.

Lycos

www.lycos.co.uk

Lycos is much more than just a search engine. It provides news, features, travel, money games plus a wide range of services and specialist channels.

mail2web

www.mail2web.com

An extremely useful internet service that allows you to pick up your emails from anywhere in the world. When accessing the service, make sure you have your mail account details, and the IP address or mail server name to hand.

Metacrawler

www.metacrawler.com

If using a normal search engine is not enough for you, Metacrawler takes you one level up and searches the major search engines for you and gives you the best results.

Mirago

www.mirago.co.uk

A UK search engine. As well as the usual range of search topics and sectors you can search the UK by region.

MSN

www.msn.com

MSN has all of the great internet services under one roof; from Hotmail email to popular MSN Messenger to news, links, latest searches and a million other resources for you to discover.

Net4Nowt

www.net4nowt.com

A leading UK Internet Service Provider (ISP) directory, with news, reviews and advice. It is a good place to start learning about internet connectivity, compare offers from ISPs and spot the best deals.

Netiquette

www.etiquette.net

Netiquette is network etiquette – the do's and don'ts of online communication. This website offers helpful advice about common courtesies and behaviour while communicating with other cyberspace citizens.

Outlook and Exchange Solutions Center

www.slipstick.com

A site dealing with managing emails using Outlook. This virtual solution centre analyses Outlook's capabilities, recommends books and tutorials and sends a bi-weekly letter to all interested in enhancing the way they handle emails.

Photobucket

www.photobucket.com

Photobucket provides free image hosting. It is a good place to store the best of your digital photos and share them with friends and family.

93

Plagiarism

www.plagiarism.org

This website is helping to fight online plagiarism, a rising problem in the virtual world. You can get all of the information you need here and get involved by reporting net content cheating.

Register

www.theregister.co.uk

News, features and analysis from the world of IT and the internet are available at Register.

SpamCop

www.spamcop.com

This website helps you to fight against spam and protect your inbox. It offers suitable advice for a variety of email programmes.

Stealth Message

www.stealthmessage.com

Stealth Message is for those ultra-secret messages that need to be encrypted or to self-destruct after being read. For those with secrets to hide and the paranoid!

Think U know

www.thinkuknow.co.uk

A website providing interactive guidelines for younger children about being safe while chatting online. It is useful for parents to go through these points alongside little ones before they start using chat rooms.

Wanadoo

www.wanadoo.co.uk

This internet service has a lot to offer. From fast and reliable broadband connection to free email, chat, online photoalbums and a printing service for your digital photos to help with buiding your own website.

WatchThatPage

www.watchthatpage.com

This internet companion will keep an eye on your favourite sites and will notify you about changes on specific pages. The reports will be presented to you as an email or, even better, as a personalised web page. The good thing about this particular service is that it is still free.

Web Talk Radio Show

www.webtalkguys.com

A talk radio show in the USA promoting the internet, online technologies and website reviews.

WebMonkey

www.webmonkey.com

WebMonkey is a fun way to build your own website. A web developer's resource that caters for everyone from beginners to advanced users.

Webuser Magazine

www.webuser.co.uk

One of the UK's best internet magazines, with all of the latest news, views and developments.

WindowsSecurity

www.windowsecurity.com

A collection of helpful articles, links and tutorials about Windows Security topics and the latest related developments and updates.

Working to Halt Online Abuse

www.haltabuse.org

Cyber-stalking, or online harassment, is a reality and WHOA's mission is to educate the internet community about the problem and encourage people to take part in creating a safe online community for everybody.

Yahoo!

www.yahoo.co.uk

Yahoo has one of the world's premier directories, large and easy to navigate. Specialist services include free email, Yahoo Messenger, latest news, weather reports and just about everything else you can think of.

Internet Fun

Now for some fun! People of all ages can download games or play online, send hilarious e-cards, read funny magazines or take part in trivia competitions. As games and graphics improve, and net connections become better and faster, so the online game experience grows and develops.

Adrenaline Vault

Aha Jokes

Animation Express

BBC Comedy

Beanotown

Birthday Alarm

Bonus

Cool Quiz

Crossword Puzzles

Danger Here

Day Free Press

Disney Online

Dumb Laws

Emily Strange

FlowGo

Fortean Times

FreakyDreams

Fun Trivia

Funny

GameHippo

GameHouse

GameSpy Arcade

GameZone Online

Guardian Notes and Queries

Guessmaster

Happy Puppy

Hattrick

House of Cards

Internet Chess Club

iSketch

JigZone

Keenspot

Kid Wizard

Kids Crosswords

Kidtastic

Mind Sports Worldwide

Mr Men

Murphy's Laws

Museum of Hoaxes

Nickelodeon

OnlineComics

Planet Quake

PlayStation

PopCap Games

Prankbot

Regards

Scrabble

Sega

Shockwave

Sony Online Entertainment

Strange Reports

SwapitShop

Teen-Scene

Thinks

Toilet Museum

Ugliest Cars in Britain

Wacky Uses

Wicked 4 Kids

Wonka

Yahoo Games

Zone

Adrenaline Vault

www.avault.com

A comprehensive online magazine with independent information about PC and video games, films and DVDs.

Aha Jokes

www.ahajokes.com

This website has thousands of clean jokes, funny pictures, funny videos and audios, cartoons and lots more.

Animation Express

www.wired.com/animation

A fascinating and entertaining collection of some of the most innovative and witty animations on the web.

BBC Comedy

www.bbc.co.uk/comedy

Comedy pages from the BBC with news, reviews, guides and a comedy blog with links, gossip other fun stuff.

Beanotown

www.beanotown.com

The online home of the one of the UK's favourite comics – Beano. The website has lots of games and activities featuring Dennis the Menace, Minnie the Minx, Gnasher, the Bash Street Kids and the other Beano characters.

Birthday Alarm

www.birthdayalarm.com

Forget about forgetting people's birthdays. Once details are entered into this site, it will email you a reminder a week before each birthday. You can keep a personal calendar here too.

Bonus

www.bonus.com

A protected site for young persons with a superb selection of great games, puzzles and lots more including art and homework help.

Cool Quiz

www.coolquiz.com

Trivia, quizzes, trivia, puzzles, trivia, humour . . . and more trivia are all on this website. Find out just how much irrelevant junk is stored in your brain.

Crossword Puzzles

www.crossword-puzzles.co.uk

A collection of interactive English crossword puzzles from sites around the world, divided into categories such as cryptic and educational.

Danger Here

www.dangerhere.com

A side-splitting site dedicated to the nonsense and drivel produced by some sports commentators. It has guff, gaffes and gobbledegook galore.

Day Free Press

www.dayfreepress.com

The online comics network. A great collection of top-quality webcomics here for your entertainment.

Disney Online

www.disney.go.com

The site where children can find out about the world of Disney.

Dumb Laws

www.dumblaws.com

An amusing insight into silly and plain crazy laws, many of which have never been repealed.

Emily Strange

www.emilystrange.com

Emily Strange is your guide here. On this website you can play some of her strange games and explore her strange world. But be very aware – this site is definitely strange.

FlowGo

www.flowgo.com

Greetings, pictures, humour, games, pictures – just a whole bundle of fun things to see and do on this website.

Fortean Times

www.forteantimes.com

The oldest 'alternative' news service on the web. It is sometimes odd, often very funny, never boring. You can get involved and submit your own stories.

FreakyDreams

www.freakydreams.com

Your dreams interpreted . . . well, perhaps. Make sure you remember every detail of your dream, then write it down and hey presto, there is an explanation for everything on Freaky Dreams.

Fun Trivia

www.funtrivia.com

Test your knowledge at FunTrivia, which claims to be the world's largest trivia site. There are over 50,000 quizzes here in nearly 8,000 categories, totalling 640,000 questions.

Funny

www.funny.co.uk

A serious guide to humour. This website has stories, news, jokes, reviews, stand-up, films, television, books, writers, radio, comedy on the web and more.

GameHippo

www.gamehippo.com

GameHippo is possibly the world's largest source of free PC games. There are over 1,000 freeware PC games to download here and all are thoroughly reviewed.

GameHouse

www.gamehouse.com

Register at this website to play loads of games online and to get the latest information about new games, and an invitation to test them. It has puzzle games, word games, arcade games and more.

GameSpy Arcade

www.gamespyarcade.com

Register at this website and play online against thousands of other players from all over the world.

GameZone Online

www.gamezone.com

A magazine with reliable, unbiased information about PC and video games. You can read the latest news and reviews, share your knowledge, download demos and more.

Guardian Notes and Queries

www.guardian.co.uk/ notesandqueries

The electronic version of Notes and Queries, the cult Guardian column where readers waste their time answering bizarre, perverse and often totally pointless questions.

Guessmaster

www.guessmaster.com

Internet guessing games for all ages, where you match your wits with artificial intelligence to see if you can think of an object, person or animal that the computer doesn't know.

Happy Puppy

www.happypuppy.com

The place to be if you want to know more about electronic, video and computer games. This online publication keeps up to date with the latest in the industry. It has good demos and freebies as well.

Hattrick

www.hattrick.org

The online football manager game where you can compete against other 'dream team' managers from around the world.

House of Cards

www.thehouseofcards.com

This site features traditional and family card games. You can learn new games, download software and play games online.

Internet Chess Club

www.chessclub.com

If you're serious about playing chess then this is the site for you. You can play games and get a rating, watch grandmasters play, take a chess lesson and more – all online.

iSketch

www.isketch.net

The online version of Pictionary, where you pit your artistic skills against other players. It is safe fun for all the family.

JigZone

www.jigzone.com

This website has free online jigsaw puzzles to suit all ages and skill levels. You can also transform your own photos into puzzles here.

Keenspot

www.keenspot.com

A publisher of exclusive webcomics sorted by category. A good place to visit and take your time.

Kid Wizard

www.kidwizard.com

A fun, educational site where children aged 6 to 12 can play games, solve mysteries, join in an interactive story and do all sorts of virtual magic.

Kids Crosswords

www.kidcrosswords.com

This website has crosswords, puzzles and strategy games for kids.

Kidtastic

www.kidtastic.com

Kidtastic has cool reviews, contests and e-cards along with a specially designed search engine to answer children's questions.

Mind Sports Worldwide

www.msoworld.com

Run by the organisers of the Mind Sports Olympiad, this site includes news, articles, an e-zine, board games, card games and puzzles – all designed to keep your mind sharp.

Mr Men

www.mrmen.com

This website includes loads of interactive fun with all the Mr Men (and Little Miss) characters.

Murphy's Laws

www.murphys-laws.com

Claiming that Murphy's Law ('If anything can go wrong it will') was born at Edwards Air Force Base, USA, in 1949, this site lists Murphy's Laws in one place. The most quoted laws are neatly ordered into more than 25 categories.

Museum of Hoaxes

www.museumofhoaxes.com

A fascinating history of hoaxes from the seventeenth century until the present day.

Incredible stories of tricks played on people or bizarre things that people have been talked into believing over the years are on this website.

Nickelodeon

www.nick.co.uk

Chat, games and other activities from Nickelodeon, plus information about their programmes.

OnlineComics

www.onlinecomics.net

This website claims to be the largest collection of online comics in existence, with over 2,300 comics divided into 20 categories.

Planet Quake

www.planetquake.com

A truly entertaining site where you can share information about the latest games, read reviews and have a go at trying different game levels.

PlayStation

www.uk.playstation.com

The latest games, news and forums, previews and reviews from Playstation.

PopCap Games

www.popcap.com

Online, downloadable and portable games – all for free from this website.

Prankbot

www.prankbot.com

Internet-based practical jokes and pranks. Ask the pranksters here to play an internet joke on one of your friends.

Regards

www.regards.com

A huge online greeting cards site that caters for all occasions and events. Additional services available include games, online chat, printing services, a reminder service and a lot more.

Scrabble

www.scrabble.com

Wars with words! Take part in an online battle, read about the history of Scrabble, discover new versions of the game or use the word checker.

Sega

www.sega.com

Sega's online presence is worth a look. Visit the site for plenty of information about the games, pretty cartoons and videos.

Shockwave

www.shockwave.com

A broad selection of well presented games for all ages, good animation and neat site design.

Sony Online Entertainment

www.station.sony.com

Sony's online games site is well designed and very popular.

Strange Reports

www.strangereports.com

On this website you will find fake news reports, trick websites and other clever pranks to play on your friends and enemies.

101

SwapitShop

www.webswappers.com

At Swap it Shop you can safely exchange the things you don't want for things you do. It teaches kids and teens the value of their possessions.

Teen-Scene

www.teen-scene.com

Teen-Scene offers pen pals, music, films, games plus useful teen links and advice too. A US site with simple design but good content.

Thinks

www.thinks.com

An extensive collection of family-friendly games, puzzles and quizzes. This website is educational as well as entertaining.

Toilet Museum

www.toiletmuseum.com

An online-museum focused on genuine toilet humour. It contains a fascinating history of the Mens Room, the Ladies Room, the Little Room, the Rest Room or wherever else you spend a penny.

Ugliest Cars in Britain

www.uglycars.co.uk

Hideous looking cars are listed on this website and given a 'paper bag rating' for the number of paper bags you should wear before accepting a ride in each particular car.

Wacky Uses

www.wackyuses.com

Discover from this website what extraordinary things you can do with ordinary products. It also has lots of weird stories and bizarre facts about everyday products.

Wicked 4 Kids

www.wicked4kids.com

Fun, interactive puzzles, brainteasers, jokes and riddles for young minds are all available on this website which provides safe and stimulating play in a safe environment for older primary school children.

Wonka

www.wonka.com

An interactive site with a huge range of interesting and entertaining things to do with space, animals, inventions and a whole lot more. It is great fun with lots to learn.

Yahoo Games

http://games.yahoo.com

The games section of the huge Yahoo site has games to suit all tastes and ages and you can play against others online too.

Zone

www.zone.com

This is Microsoft's games zone. It offers card and board games, puzzles plus action and simulation games.

Languages

The internet hosts billions of web pages in all languages. The best search engines are capable of translating whole websites, making global communication fast and easy. You can take advantage of free learning resources online, find out where to purchase learning software and materials, get help with the National Curriculum language of your choice, practise your language skills by reading a foreign newspaper, find a teacher or course, or just do some vocabulary training exercises. Useful sites for beginners through to translators are also featured here.

About.com – French

About.com – German

About.com – Latin

Babelfish

BBC Languages

BUBL Link – Gaelic Language

Chinese Languages

CNNenEspanol

don Quijote

El Pais Online

EnglishClub

Ethnologue

European Parliament

French Assistant

French Revision

From Language to Language

German For Travellers

Google – Language Tools

GUT!

iLoveLanguages

Jacques Leon's French Language Course

Japanese Language and Culture Resource Community

JUMA – Das Jugendmagazin

LanguageGames

Languages Online

Latin Library

Le Monde Online

Learn German through Fairy Tales

Learn Spanish

Lingu@net Europa

Lingua Central

Linguascope

Lost in Translation

MFL Games

National Advisory Centre on Early
  Language Learning

National Centre for Languages

Omniglot

Scottish Language Dictionaries

Sowieso

Spiegel Online

Tecla

Vocabulary Training Exercises

Your Dictionary

ZUT!

L 104

About.com – French

www.french.about.com

A teaching and learning resource and an extra helping of information about French people and culture.

About.com – German

www.german.about.com

This website provides grammar, vocabulary, word of the day, articles and guides about German language and culture.

About.com – Latin

www.ancienthistory.about.com/cs/latingrammar

A comprehensive resource to help learn the rules behind the Latin language. It includes the formation of word endings, grammar, adjectives, adverbs and cases.

Babelfish

www.babelfish.altavista.com

The veteran online translation service. You can use it as a dictionary but also to translate whole websites.

BBC Languages

www.bbc.co.uk/languages

Test your French or Spanish knowledge by reading or listening to some BBC news, take an online course, or brush up on holiday phrases. There is lots here for language students at every level. Another brilliant site from the BBC.

BUBL Link – Gaelic Language

http://bubl.ac.uk/link/g/gaeliclanguage.htm

An internet resource about the Gaelic language including library material. It is a useful starting point for anyone interested in this language and its history.

Chinese Languages

www.chinalanguage.com

An introspective into the world and history of Chinese languages. A well documented, resourceful site.

CNNenEspanol

www.cnnespanol.com

Improve your Spanish comprehension through reading the day's news in Spanish on this website.

don Quijote

www.donquijote.org

Apart from tons of free learning tutorials, this site hosts a lot of information about Spanish culture, travel advice, music and books.

El Pais Online

www.elpais.es

The online version of the leading Spanish newspaper. You can read the articles to improve your Spanish comprehension.

EnglishClub

www.englishclub.net

Aimed at students learning English as a second language and also useful for teachers teaching English, this site is full of good quality, free resources.

Ethnologue

www.ethnologue.com

A fascinating website about the languages of the world. Ethnologue's comprehensive database offers a wealth of information about languages and their history. If you are interested in the origins of languages then this site is a must.

European Parliament

www.europarl.eu.int

On this website you can click on the language of your choice and then read all about European issues. It is an excellent way to improve your language comprehension skills.

French Assistant

www.frenchassistant.com

Learn and practice your French knowledge using online tutorials and lessons and make use of more than 10,000 sound samples to brush up on your pronunciation.

French Revision

www.frenchrevision.co.uk

Tons of interactive exercises in French – listening, reading or writing – for students aged 11 to 18. Do the online tests and see what score you get.

From Language to Language

www.langtolang.com

From Language to Languate offers basic translation from English into more than 10 other languages. Specialist translation software and gadgets are also available online.

German For Travellers

www.germanfortravellers.com

Basic German language tutorials along with resources to highlight German culture are available on this website.

Google – Language Tools

www.google.com/language_tools

Google offers a search facility for web pages written in more than 35 languages. You can also translate texts and web pages here or set your Google search facility to a language of your choice.

L 105

GUT!

http://gut.languageskills.co.uk

An interactive resource for German teachers and learners following the national curriculum. There are stacks of exercises split into year groups. Its sister site ZUT! covers French.

iLoveLanguages

www.ilovelanguages.com

A US site with a major collection of internet sources relating to a wide variety of languages.

Jacques Leon's French Language Course

www.jump-gate.com/languages/french/

This easy-to-follow course is intended to enable you to understand written French from newspapers, magazines, road signs, etc. and to write a letter to a French friend.

Japanese Language and Culture Resource Community

www.japanese-online.com

A good starting point for learning about Japan and Japanese language. Multimedia language lessons, an online dictionary and a discussion forum are just some of this website's features.

JUMA – Das Jugendmagazin

www.juma.de

An online magazine aimed at teenagers learning German. It is not just a good way to improve your understanding of the language as the magazine also gives an insight into German youth culture.

LanguageGames

www.languagegames.org

On this website you can play while learning foreign languages. The games include crosswords, search the word games or hangman in English, Spanish, French, German or Italian.

Languages Online

www.languagesonline.org.uk

Developed by a teacher, this invaluable site hosts excellent language exercises in French, German, Spanish and Italian.

Latin Library

www.thelatinlibrary.com

A collection of Latin texts, from the classical to the modern.

Le Monde Online

www.lemonde.fr

The online version of France's most well-known daily newspaper. Reading the articles is a great way to practice and improve your French comprehension.

Learn German through Fairy Tales

http://faculty.acu.edu/~goebeld/maerchen/maermenu.htm

The idea here is to learn German through Fairy Tales, supplied by the Gutenberg Collection. It includes help with vocabulary and grammar.

Learn Spanish

www.studyspanish.com

Online Spanish tutorials, tapes, CDs, home study courses, travellers' notes and a directory of language schools, all are on offer here (and most are free).

Lingu@net Europa

www.linguanet-europa.org

Lingu@net Europa is an excellent resource and support for teachers of modern languages. It provides information about, and links to, top-quality online resources from around the world devoted to the teaching of modern languages.

Lingua Central

www.linguacentral.co.uk

A huge collection of free online resources for learning French, Spanish or German, from primary to age 18.

Linguascope

www.linguascope.com

Language resources and activities online in English, French, Italian, German and Spanish. The affordable subscriptions allow teachers and students to access the full range of products.

Lost in Translation

www.tashian.com/multibabel

One to visit if you need a break from serious language study. This website translates texts into different languages, consecutively, and then back into English with hilarious and interesting results.

MFL Games

www.mflgames.co.uk

At MFL Games you can play free online games to learn French, Spanish or German. It provides an easy way to learn the basics and more.

National Advisory Centre on Early Language Learning

www.nacell.org.uk

A Department for Education Skills initiative to promote and develop the provision and quality of modern foreign language learning at primary schools.

National Centre for Languages

www.cilt.org.uk

Find out about the work of the National Centre for Languages, the Government-funded centre of expertise on languages. The Centre's aim is to promote a greater capability in languages across all sectors of society in the UK.

Omniglot

www.omniglot.com

A fascinating directory looking at the origins of over 200 writing systems from around the world. A wonderful site for anyone interested in how writing has evolved.

Scottish Language Dictionaries

www.snda.org.uk

An interactive site promoting the languages of Scotland. Scottish spelling and grammar, recommended reading and notes about the history of the Scottish language.

Sowieso

www.sowieso.de

Sowieso is a collection of newspapers edited for young German readers. Reading the articles is an ideal way to practice your German comprehension.

Spiegel Online

www.spiegel.de

The online version of one of Germany's best newspapers. You can improve your German comprehension by reading the articles.

Tecla

www.sgci.mec.es/uk/Pub/tecla.html

The online text magazine for Spanish learners and teachers.

Vocabulary Training Exercises

www.vokabel.com

Online vocabulary exercises in French, Spanish, German and English. You can create your own test or follow the ready-made ones available.

Your Dictionary

www.yourdictionary.com

A language products and services company that claims its website has 'the most comprehensive and authoritative language portal on the web'. It contains over 2,500 dictionaries and grammars in over 300 languages.

ZUT!

www.zut.org.uk

An interactive resource for French teachers and learners, following the national curriculum. More than 1000 exercises available online and are split into sections at beginner, intermediate and advanced level.

Lifestyle and Fashion

Fashion and beauty, celebrity news and gossip together with information on how to lead a healthy lifestyle are covered in this section. How to lose weight, eat organic, deal with allergies, the NHS online, health advice for teenagers and issues such as contraception and embarrassing problems, are all included here.

All Allergy	Fashion and Textile Museum
Astrology.com – Teen	Fashion UK
Avert	Femail
BBC Teens	Food Forum
Beauty Worlds	Glamour
British Nutrition Foundation	Hair Archives
Brook	Handbag
Celebhoo	Health Sites
Children First	Hello!
Connexions	Hint Fashion Magazine
Cooking By Numbers	Internet Health Library
Coolmeals	LifeBytes
Costume Gallery	Likeitis
Dr. Weil	Malehealth
Eating Disorders Association	Mind, Body and Soul
ELLE.com	Museum of Costume
Embarrassing Problems	Mykindaplace.com

NHS Direct Online

Organicfood

SharpMan

SmartGirl

Solemates – The Century in Shoes

Stressbusting

Student Health

Supermodels

Surgery Door

Teenage Health Freak

Teenage Pregnancy Unit

Teensforum

TeenToday

TheSite

Think about Drink

Three Fat Chicks

UKTV Food

Vegetarian Society

VegWeb

Virtual HairCare

Vogue

Youth2Youth

Zoom V

L 110

All Allergy

www.allallergy.net

A portal to allergy, asthma and intolerance information on the internet. All Allergy contains a wealth of resources for both healthcare professionals and consumers. If you suffer from any allergy, you'll find this site useful.

Astrology.com – Teen

www.teen.astrology.com

Don't start your day without checking what the stars have in store for you today! Alternatively, on this website you can check your romantic sun sign profile or find out who's your best match.

Avert

www.avert.org

HIV/AIDS is a reality that can't be ignored. Learn about the virus, its transmission, testing, how to stay safe, treatment, care and much more on this very helpful site.

BBC Teens

www.bbc.co.uk/teens

The BBC's site for teenagers looks into a variety of subjects of interest to girls and boys. It is easy to browse with a good mix of fun and serious information.

Beauty Worlds

www.beautyworlds.com

Going behind the make-up and the glitz, Beauty World explores what people and cultures around the world find beautiful and why.

British Nutrition Foundation

www.nutrition.org.uk

All aspects of nutrition are covered here, with a particular emphasis on nutrition for children and teenagers.

Brook

www.brook.org.uk

Brook provides sexual health and contraception advice for under 25s. Their website contains lots of useful information and explains how you can contact them for further help and guidance.

Celebhoo

www.celebhoo.com

Entertaining fan site with lots of chat and gossip and featuring reviewed links to celebrity fan sites.

Children First

www.childrenfirst.nhs.uk

A website where youngsters and teens can find out about their health, connect with others around the world, share views on life and health issues, get the latest celebrity gossip and obtain help with health problems.

Connexions

www.connexions.gov.uk

Are you aged 13–19 and living in England? Connexions provides help and advice on learning, careers, health, relationships, money and much more.

Cooking By Numbers

www.cookingbynumbers.com

Just feed in details of what is left in your cupboard and fridge and Cooking By Numbers will provide a selection of recipes. A pity it won't do the cooking too!

Coolmeals

www.coolmeals.co.uk

Cool facts about food and children, and activities that involve food and the trendy topic of nutrition are all available on this website.

Costume Gallery

www.costumegallery.com

Dedicated to images of fashion with over 25,000 images of fashion and costume going back to the early 1800s. Online classes showing how to make some of these costumes are also available.

Dr. Weil

www.drweil.com

A provider of online information and products for optimum health. The website also has advice on balanced living, vitamins and lots more.

Eating Disorders Association

www.edauk.com

A website providing information and help for people with eating disorders, such as anorexia, bulimia and binge eating.

ELLE.com

www.elle.com

ELLE.com complements the famous magazine that focuses on fashion, beauty and style.

Embarrassing Problems

www.embarrassingproblems.co.uk

A website helping to deal with health problems that are difficult to discuss with anyone.

Fashion and Textile Museum

www.ftmlondon.org

The first museum in the UK dedicated to contemporary fashion and textiles, inaugurated in 2003. The museum aims to educate the audience in all areas of fashion and textile design.

Fashion UK

www.fuk.co.uk

The best of UK fashion with news, features, photos, designer interviews and forums.

Femail

www.femail.co.uk

A magazine for girls and women from the Daily Mail covering fashion, beauty, health, showbiz, horoscopes, lifestyle and stacks more.

Food Forum

www.foodforum.org.uk

A super site with worksheets, homework and other resources covering food, diet and health issues for young persons, parents and teachers. Its content has been approved by the National Grid for Learning.

Glamour

www.glamourmagazine.co.uk

The website that complements Glamour magazine. It has fashion, beauty tips, and, of course, chat and gossip about celebrities.

Hair Archives

www.hairarchives.com

A website devoted to vintage hair fashion. A library of beautiful (and sometimes bizarre) hairstyles from years gone by.

Handbag

www.handbag.com

Handbag holds just about everything including beauty, fashion, health, fitness, relationships, celebrity gossip, family issues and lots more.

Health Sites

www.healthsites.co.uk

An extremely useful, independent portal site for both non-medical people and healthcare professionals, bringing together websites that provide reliable health information. Primarily UK sites are listed.

Hello!

www.hellomagazine.com

Complementing the famous magazine, Hello! This site is for those who can't live without knowing what the world's rich and famous are wearing, who they are marrying, what clubs and restaurants they frequent and where they spend their holidays.

Hint Fashion Magazine

www.hintmag.com

A classy online magazine with great photography, news and features from the world of fashion and modelling.

Internet Health Library

www.internethealthlibrary.com

An attractive and informative site that claims to be the UK's largest online resource for complementary therapy, alternative medicine and natural healthcare.

LifeBytes

www.lifebytes.gov.uk

Approved by the National Grid for Learning and aimed at young people aged 11 to 14, this site is packed with loads of information about leading a healthy life. Friendly and colourful and presented in a fun and interesting way, LifeBytes is a good companion for kids who want to learn more about health.

Likeitis

www.likeitis.org.uk

This website provides information for young people about all aspects of teenage life and sex education. Topics that are told 'like it is' include peer pressure, puberty, periods, contraception, teenage pregnancy and much more.

Malehealth

www.malehealth.co.uk

From Men's Health Forum, the leading men's health charity, Malehealth provides essential information about key health problems that affect men and down-to-earth tips and advice to help men lead a healthier life.

Mind, Body and Soul

www.mindbodysoul.gov.uk

A website giving young people aged 14–16 the lowdown on health in a fun and interesting way. Covering a range of health topics Mind, Body and Soul is jam-packed with useful advice.

Museum of Costume

www.museumofcostume.co.uk

The Museum of Costume in Bath houses one of the world's finest collections of fashionable dress and fashion accessories. It has great online resources for anyone interested in the history of fashion.

Mykindaplace.com

www.mykindaplace.com

A popular online magazine that caters for teenagers' needs. There is a bit of everything in here from fashion to chat, games to stories that make you cringe, an agony aunt always on call and online competitions with cool prizes.

NHS Direct Online

www.nhsdirect.nhs.uk

An informative guide to healthcare in the UK, from the National Health Service. There are also features on healthcare concerns for teenagers and guidance on issues such as stopping smoking. The website also includes a 'listen here' section where you can listen to 200+ clips on health topics.

Organicfood

www.organicfood.co.uk

An online magazine with facts, information and opinions about organic food.

L113

SharpMan

www.sharpman.com

An online magazine that is the ultimate 'how to' guide for men covering grooming, wardrobe, dating, travel, health, consumer issues and much more. An A–Z to being sharp.

SmartGirl

www.smartgirl.org

This is a web resource and forum for smart girls. You can share your thoughts with other smart girls, consult the fortune teller, review books, magazines and films or just have some fun.

Solemates – The Century in Shoes

www.centuryinshoes.com

A beautifully designed site that looks at the history of footwear in the twentieth century, decade by decade, using audio and video footage.

Stressbusting

www.stressbusting.co.uk

A website all about stress – and how to beat it. Stress is considered by many to be the 'epidemic of the age' and this site provides information about stress symptoms, therapies and relief in an easy-to-follow manner.

Student Health

www.studenthealth.co.uk

Over 220 printable advice leaflets on topical health issues aimed at young people are available from this website.

Supermodels

www.supermodels.com

Submit your photo to this website and let the world decide if you stand a chance as a supermodel.

Surgery Door

www.surgerydoor.co.uk

A huge website with health advice for all ages, the latest medical research and special sections dedicated to children's health.

Teenage Health Freak

www.teenagehealth.org

This website provides accurate and reliable health information for teenagers, presented in a colourful, entertaining and contemporary manner.

Teenage Pregnancy Unit

www.teenagepregnancyunit.gov.uk

The Teenage Pregnancy Unit provides information about the government's teenage pregnancy strategy. If you are a teenager looking for advice on sexual health or pregnancy issues, or a parent seeking information on talking to your teenagers about sex, there are also links here to many useful sites.

Teensforum

www.teensforum.com

A US online magazine and forum for teenage girls covering health and fitness, entertainment, family, fashion, beauty, fun, relationships and school.

TeenToday

www.teentoday.co.uk

A free online teen chat community plus fashion trends and recommendations and all in one place.

TheSite

www.thesite.org

Billed as a 'guide to the real world', TheSite aims to give quality, impartial information and advice for young adults, aged 16 to 25. They provide the facts so that young people can make informed decisions.

Think about Drink

www.wrecked.co.uk

A website providing straightforward advice for young people about the damage caused by alcohol consumption.

Three Fat Chicks

www.3fatchicks.com

This website has stacks of practical tips for those wishing to lose weight. There are diet reviews, articles, nutrition guides, recipes, fitness tips and much more from '3 fat chicks on a diet'.

UKTV Food

www.uktvfood.co.uk

This website features recipes, cook books and information from programmes featured on UKTV Food, the television channel celebrating fine food and the nation's favourite chefs.

Vegetarian Society

www.vegsoc.org

Recipes, information about health and nutrition and cooking classes are all available on this website. A visit to this site is a must for all vegetarians or those thinking of going vegetarian.

VegWeb

www.vegweb.com

Useful information for vegans and vegetarians is available from this website. Recipes, cookbooks, newsletters and links to other interesting sites are just some of this site's features.

Virtual HairCare

www.virtualhaircare.com

An online haircare magazine showcasing the latest looks. It is packed with tips, guidance and advice on every aspect of hair care and hair fashion.

Vogue

www.vogue.co.uk

The well known fashion magazine, online.

Youth2Youth

www.youth2youth.co.uk

A unique telephone, email and online chat helpline service run for young people by young people.

Zoom V

www.zoom.co.uk

An online fashion magazine covering trends, special offers and the latest news.

Maths

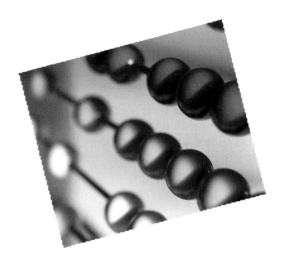

This category includes a whole range of resources across the spectrum of this complex subject. As well as several websites covering the National Curriculum for GCSE and A Level students, there is valuable support and advice from maths tutors and maths forums. There are sites here to help students with their homework or to improve their existing knowledge, including some interactive, fun ways to get the message across.

1000 Problems to Enjoy

AAA Math

a-maths.com

Association of Teachers of Mathematics

BBC Schools

Constants and Equations Pages

Coolmath4kids

Count On

Dartmaths

Easymaths

Echalk.co.uk

ExploreLearning

Figure This Maths

Funbrain

Interactive Maths Miscellany and Puzzles

Isaac Newton Institute for Mathematical
    Sciences

Kumon Maths and English

MacTutor History of Mathematics
    Archive

Math Forum

Math.com

Mathematical Association

Maths Alive

A Maths Dictionary for Kids

Maths is Fun

Maths Online

MathsNet

MathWorld

Mrs Glosser's Math Goodies

MyMaths

Newton's Window

Nrich Online Maths Club

Primary Maths

QuickMath

SOS MATHematics

Tuckermaths

Virtual Textbook

Waldo's Interactive Maths Pages

1000 Problems to Enjoy

www.1000Problems.com

A welcome resource for maths teachers, developed by maths teachers, with maths problems for students at all ability levels at Key Stages 3 and 4.

AAA-math

www.aaa.math.com

A US maths resource primarily aimed at Key Stage 2 and Key Stage 3.

a-maths.com

www.a-maths.com

a-maths.com offers a platform where GCSE Maths students (and their teachers and parents) can meet, interact and share views online. On this website students can pose questions to volunteer tutors, look for resources and exchange ideas and solutions and it contains a comprehensive list of maths websites.

Association of Teachers of Mathematics

www.atm.org.uk

The website of the association that aims to support and encourage the teaching and learning of mathematics. Maths resources are reviewed here and special offers and services are available for members.

BBC Schools

www.bbc.co.uk/schools

The usual top quality site from the BBC, providing learning resources for school and home. The maths material is suitable for students aged 11 to 16.

Constants and Equations Pages

www.tcaep.co.uk

This website is split into three main categories covering science, maths and astronomy. The constants and equations are at hand to help with algebra, trigonometry, calculus, mathematical symbols and a lot more.

Coolmath4kids

www.coolmath4kids.com

An attractive site that makes learning maths fun (honest!) through great interactive games and puzzles. It has been correctly described as 'an amusement park of maths and more'.

Count On

www.counton.org

A comprehensive and wide-ranging maths resource for teachers and pupils. There's lots here including fun with numbers, games, a virtual maths museum, a maths magazine and help for students preparing for GCSE and 'A' level exams.

Dartmaths

www.dartmaths.co.uk

An excellent and well proven maths resource with lessons and tracking of pupil progress. It includes exercises with soundtracks.

Easymaths

www.easymaths.com

Help is available here on Easymaths for people who don't find mathematics fun. Give this site a chance if you hate maths, take one tutorial at a time and it will help you improve your results.

Echalk.co.uk

www.echalk.co.uk

This website is a free resource for teachers to use with interactive whiteboards and data projectors. An impressive and excellent tool for primary and secondary Science and Maths teachers using interactive whiteboards.

ExploreLearning

www.explorelearning.com

This site has a lot to offer. It is a superb interactive site with a range of modular maths and science simulations for teachers and students.

Figure This Maths

www.figurethis.org

A US site that helps families enjoy mathematics outside school through fun and engaging, high-quality challenges.

Funbrain

www.funbrain.com

An attractive, fun site that encourages learning – for all ages – through playing activities covering a wide range of subjects. Special advice for parents and teachers is also available online.

Interactive Maths Miscellany and Puzzles

www.cut-the-knot.org

The creator of this site is passionate about mathematics. This site is not just a scholar's resource but is interesting for mature students as well.

Isaac Newton Institute for Mathematical Sciences

www.newton.cam.ac.uk

You can take a peek at some serious mathematics research here involving scientists from around the world. A good website to visit if you intend to take the study of mathematics further.

Kumon Maths and English

www.kumon.co.uk

An after class teaching programme available for children of all ages and abilities. Find out from this website about the Kumon Method and where to find your nearest Kumon learning centre.

MacTutor History of Mathematics Archive

www-groups.dcs.st-and.ac.uk/history

A fascinating site where you can find out about the development of maths in different cultures throughout the ages, and famous mathematicians in history. The website was created by the School of Mathematics and Statistics at the University of St Andrews.

Math Forum

www.mathforum.org

Math Forum aims to be a leading centre for mathematics education on the internet. It provides resources, materials, activities and more, for teachers and students alike.

Math.com

www.math.com

Math.com aims to provide 'revolutionary ways for students, parents and teachers to learn maths'. There's homework help, practice, calculator, tools and games, plus an extensive set of resources.

Mathematical Association

www.m-a.org.uk

Working through its councils and committees, the Mathematical Association is geared towards improving communication between teachers and pupils and enhancing the teaching of mathematics.

Maths Alive

www.mathsalive.co.uk

MathsAlive is an entire ICT based curriculum and approach, designed to support delivery of the key stage 3 framework for teaching mathematics.

A Maths Dictionary for Kids

www.amathsdictionaryforkids.com

The beauty of this interactive dictionary is its simplicity. More than 500 common mathematical terms are explained here using simple language and great graphics.

Maths is Fun

www.mathsisfun.com

Developed by a maths teacher, the site combines the learning of mathematics with having fun. It is aimed at pupils aged between 11 and 16, the content mixes complex stuff with easy bits and has something for everyone.

Maths Online

www.mathsonline.co.uk

A comprehensive resource of high quality maths teaching materials for secondary education at all stages. This subscription site includes a resource centre, games room, worksheet library and study room.

MathsNet

www.mathsnet.net

A work of love from a mathematics teacher who has put together a lot of useful content, ending up with an entertaining, yet educative site that makes math learning fun. The interactive maths dictionary and the interactive graphs are great!

MathWorld

www.mathworld.wolfram.com

Delve into recreational mathematics or study some serious algebra or take an excursion into the foundations of mathematics. MathWorld claims to be the web's most complete mathematics resource.

Mrs Glosser's Math Goodies

www.mathgoodies.com

An attractive and easy to use site that provides free help with maths including interactive lessons, homework help, worksheets and forums. There are over 400 pages of activities.

MyMaths

www.mymaths.co.uk

An impressive subscription site for teachers and pupils offering maths guidance and full access to interactive online tools that make maths learning fun.

Newton's Window

www.newtonswindow.com

An impressive maths site for students, teachers and families with ideas, resources, links and much more.

Nrich Online Maths Club

www.nrich.maths.org.uk

About the NRICH project, based at the University of Cambridge's Faculty of Education, this site gives students the opportunity to explore mathematical ideas and offers challenging activites. A useful resource for teachers and students.

Primary Maths

www.numbergym.co.uk

Primary Maths is committed to the creation of quality numeracy software, designed to develop core numeracy concepts and skills. The emphasis throughout is on interactive participation. These activities are particularly suitable for use with interactive whiteboards.

QuickMath

www.quickmath.com

A useful, free, automated service which can answer a big variety of common maths problems.

SOS MATHematics

www.sosmath.com

An American site with heaps of material on subjects such as trigonometry, calculus, matrix algebra and differential equations. You are encouraged with your maths through practical step by step participation.

Tuckermaths

www.tuckermaths.co.uk

A versatile resource for teachers and pupils at Key Stage 2, Key Stage 3 and Key Stage 4 foundation level maths. It has been designed for use with interactive white boards and individually by pupils. The website has clear and graduated content by topic, with student tracking.

Virtual Textbook

www.virtualtextbook.fsnet.co.uk

An excellent resource for maths teachers and also for students doing their maths revision. Making use of information technology, these interactive lessons are highly visual and help make maths lessons more interesting.

Waldo's Interactive Maths Pages

www.waldomaths.com

This website is a work of love from a British maths teacher. It is a free, useful, extensive maths resource for teachers and for students aged 11 to 18.

Media

This section is a practical guide for students with an interest in the media. The sites include online news agencies and directories for national news organisations, plus multiple media resources for students taking Media Studies as part of the National Curriculum. **Visit the Television, Film and Radio category as well as Drama, Music and English for extra research material or support.**

A Level Media Studies

Anorak

AP Wide World Photos

Archives

Associated Press

BBC News

Big News Network

British Library Newspapers

British Press Awards

Broadband Music Magazine

BusinessWeek Online

CBBC Newsround

CBS News

Children's Express

CNN

Communication, Cultural and Media Studies Infobase

Country Life

Daily Express

Daily Mail

Economist

Film Education

Financial Times

Fish4News

Google News

Guardian Unlimited

Independent

Independent Radio News

ITN

Kidon Media Link

Litnotes UK

MCS

Media Studies

Media UK

Mirror

National Gallery of the Spoken Word

National Museum of Photography, Film and Television

Newsconnect

Newseum

Newspaper Society

Newspapers of the World

Online Newspapers

PA Photos

Picture Editors' Awards

Positive News

Press Association

Press Complaints Commission

Punch

Sky News

Telegraph

Times Online

What The Papers Say

Which?

ZNet

M 122

A Level Media Studies

www.start.at/mediastudies

Valuable resources are gathered together on this website by a media teacher. It provides useful links and notes and plenty of space for further developments and uses material and comments from students.

Anorak

www.anorak.co.uk

Anorak is an e-zine which was first published in 1995. The day's papers and showbiz magazines are reviewed in its own irreverent, humorous style.

AP Wide World Photos

www.apwideworld.com

With more than 800,000 photos, this is one of the largest collections of images in the world compiled by Associated Press.

Archives

www.adflip.com

A collection of internet adverts covering a whole range of sections. It is a good

introduction to advertising and the pop culture the adverts represent.

Associated Press

www.ap.org

The Associated Press or AP is the largest and oldest news organisation in the world and serves as a source of news, photos, graphics, audio and video for thousands of daily newspaper, radio, television and online customers.

BBC News

www.bbc.co.uk/news

A UK and world news website which is updated every minute.

Big News Network

www.bignewsnetwork.com

This news website collects stories, articles and editorials from publications around the world.

British Library Newspapers

**www.bl.uk/catalogues/
newspapers.html**

The British Library Newspapers' collection includes all UK national daily and Sunday newspapers from 1801 to the present, plus selected newspapers from around the world and popular periodicals covering all subjects.

British Press Awards

www.britishpressawards.com

The British Press Awards are an annual celebration of excellence in journalism.

Broadband Music Magazine

www.fmagazine.com

A good broadband connection is suggested to make the most of this superbly designed online music magazine. You can flick through its content while listening to good quality streamed music.

BusinessWeek Online

www.businessweek.com

The online version of the popular and influential US business weekly.

CBBC Newsround

www.bbc.co.uk/newsround

If you want to keep up to date with the latest news from around the world, the Newsround site is one of the best places to look. It has all the news of the day and fills you in on some of the important background behind the stories and it's all aimed at children.

CBS News

www.cbsnews.com

This website provides news from the US, plus international news from a US perspective.

Children's Express

www.childrens-express.org

A great site about Children's Express, a news agency producing stories written by young people. Through their unique programme, young people between 8 and 18 research and write stories on issues that are important to them for publication in national and local newspapers, magazines, television and radio.

CNN

www.cnn.com

This website provides news, sport, technology, health, entertainment and more – from a US perspective.

Communication, Cultural and Media Studies Infobase

www.ccms-infobase.com

The CCMS Infobase attempts to cover most of the basics of what students of communication, cultural and media studies are likely to need to know in their last couple of years of secondary education or first year at university.

Country Life

www.countrylife.co.uk

The online version of the colourful country lifestyle magazine.

Daily Express

www.express.co.uk

The website from one of the UK's most popular daily newspapers.

Daily Mail

www.dailymail.co.uk

An attractive and comprehensive news site from one of the UK's popular tabloid newspapers.

Economist

www.economist.co.uk

A great site from the top weekly magazine covering business and politics. You can access their excellent country briefings here too.

Film Education

www.filmeducation.org

A unique link between education and the film industry, facilitating the study of film and cinema across the UK national curriculum.

Financial Times

www.ft.com

The online version of the daily newspaper that specialises in economic and business news.

Fish4News

www.fish4news.co.uk

If you type in your town, county or postcode on this website, you will receive a list of links to local and regional newspaper sites.

Google News

www.google.co.uk/news

Google's news site with sections covering the UK, world, business, science, technology, sport, entertainment and health, using information from 4,500 news sources.

Guardian Unlimited

www.guardian.co.uk

The online version of the Guardian newspaper.

Independent

www.independent.co.uk

Online news, sport, analysis, education, money, travel and more from the Independent.

Independent Radio News

www.irn.co.uk

IRN is the UK and international news service that is heard by 27 million listeners to commercial radio stations across the UK.

ITN

www.itn.co.uk

One of the largest news organisations in the world, ITN produces news and other factual programmes for television, radio and news media, both for the UK and overseas.

Kidon Media Link

www.kidon.com

A directory of newspapers and news sources on the internet from around the world.

Litnotes UK

www.litnotes.co.uk

A website offering free resources for A/S and A2 media studies, English language and literature students.

MCS

www.aber.ac.uk/media

A great resource for media students, this is an award-winning portal to sites that are useful for the study of media and communication.

Media Studies

www.robertsmyth.co.uk/media

This website offers material for A level and GCSE media studies, produced by the media department of the Robert Smyth school. It has lots of links to other websites too.

Media UK

www.mediauk.com

The independent media directory for the UK listing nearly 1,400 newspapers, over 1,300 magazines, 650 radio stations and 350+ television channels.

Mirror

www.mirror.co.uk

The online version of the daily tabloid newspaper.

National Gallery of the Spoken Word

www.ngsw.org

The NGSW is creating an online digital library of spoken word collections spanning the twentieth century and covering a wide variety of topics.

National Museum of Photography, Film and Television

www.nmpft.org.uk

It is not just the exhibited items in the museum, based in Bradford, that attract visitors. This great website's educational pages have extensive and interesting tutorials and advice.

Newsconnect

www.newsconnect.net

Newsconnect contains pictorial links connecting to websites of newspapers and other media organisations. They are mainly US media but there are links to UK and international media too.

Newseum

www.newseum.org

The world's first 'interactive museum of news'. The features include 'Today's Front Pages' from newspapers around the world. The website is updated daily.

Newspaper Society

www.newspapersoc.org.uk

The Newspaper Society is the voice of the UK's regional press, representing and promoting the interests of over 1300 titles – regional, local, daily and weekly. Their website includes a directory of links to newspaper sites around the country.

Newspapers of the World

www.actualidad.com

A directory of newspapers from around the world with links to their sites.

Online Newspapers

www.onlinenewspapers.com

A simple portal site that links to thousands of online newspapers and magazines from around the world.

PA Photos

www.paphotos.com

PA Photos is the photographic arm of The Press Association providing collections of news, entertainment, sport and celebrity pictures for publication.

Picture Editors' Awards

www.pictureawards.net

The Picture Editors' Awards recognise and reward the very best of photographic journalism throughout the UK and Ireland.

Positive News

www.positivenews.org.uk

The online version of Positive News, an alternative newspaper that reports on issues rarely covered by the mainstream media including people, events and influences that help create a positive future.

Press Association

www.pa.press.net

PA is a leading provider of news and sports information and pictures to newspapers, broadcasters and online publishers around the UK.

Press Complaints Commission

www.pcc.org.uk

The PCC deals with complaints from the public about the editorial content of newspapers and magazines.

Punch

www.punch.co.uk

Punch magazine has been satirising and lampooning the British establishment since 1841. A website for those who like their laughs to come with a good deal of thought.

Sky News

www.skynews.co.uk

Up-to-the-minute news from Sky including UK and world news, business, showbiz, money and more.

Telegraph

www.telegraph.co.uk

A comprehensive news service from the well-established UK daily broadsheet newspaper.

Times Online

www.timesonline.co.uk

The online news from The Times which is widely regarded as one of the best informed news services.

What The Papers Say

www.whatthepaperssay.co.uk

'The quick fix for busy news junkies.' This website contains edited highlights from the UK's daily papers.

Which?

www.which.net

The website of the UK's leading consumer magazine. If you want to know about the best buys, obtain the latest product reports, check brand reliability or avoid the worst services then visit this publication's website.

ZNet

www.zmag.org/weluser.htm

Possibly the world's foremost radical comment site, ZNet describes itself as 'a community of people committed to social change'.

Museums

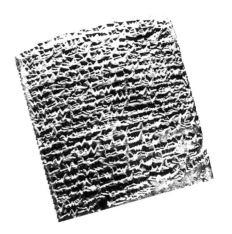

This is one of the most important education portals. On these websites you can enjoy virtual visits to the world's famous museums. You will find links to museums in the UK and around the world in this category. There are also unusual museums to visit and many of the sites included provide valuable information for coursework, projects, general knowledge, as well as that special ingredient – inspiration. **The Art category may also hold further relevant information.**

24 Hour Museum

British Museum

Chinese Art Museums and Galleries

Collect Britain

Geffrye Museum

Guggenheim Museum

Imperial War Museum

Indian Museum, India

Kyoto National Museum, Japan

London Canal Museum

London Transport Museum

Museum in Docklands

Museum of Garden History

Museum of London

Museum Stuff

Museums and Galleries

Museums of Britain

Museums on the Web

National Army Museum

National Maritime Museum

National Railway Museum

Natural History Museum

Old Operating Theatre

Petrie Museum of Egyptian Archaeology

RAF Museum

Science Museum

Smithsonian Institution

State Hermitage Museum

Thackray Museum

Uffizi Gallery

Vatican

Victoria and Albert Museum

Virtual Library Museums Pages

24 Hour Museum

www.24hourmuseum.org.uk

The UK's 'national virtual museum' is a gateway to over 2,500 museums, galleries and heritage associations across the country. It is twinned with www.show.me.uk which is designed for children.

British Museum

www.thebritishmuseum.ac.uk

The British Museum houses one of the world's finest, and largest, collections of art and antiquities from both ancient and living cultures. They have an extensive online presence with useful educational resources.

Chinese Art Museums and Galleries

www.chinapage.com/museum.html

This website provides links to museums and art galleries around the world with online presentations of their Chinese collections.

Collect Britain

www.collectbritain.co.uk

On this website you can view and hear over 100,000 images and sounds from the British Library's world-renowned collections, all without leaving your home or school.

Geffrye Museum

www.geffrye-museum.org.uk

At this London museum you can peek through the keyhole into the past and see period rooms showing the changing style of English domestic interiors from 1600 to the present day. There are good online resources including a virtual tour.

Guggenheim Museum

www.guggenheim.org

The attractive website of the world-famous Guggenheim Museum of modern art, which now has operations in Bilbao, Las Vegas, Venice and Berlin as well as its original home in New York.

Imperial War Museum

www.iwm.org.uk

The Imperial War Museum in London encourages the understanding and study of modern warfare and war-time experiences. Its exhibits range from tanks and aircraft to personal letters and ration books, films, photographs and sound recordings.

Indian Museum, India

www.indianmuseum-calcutta.org

The Indian Museum in Kolkata (Calcutta) is the oldest institution of its kind in the Asia Pacific region. Established in 1814 it has over 60 galleries covering art, archaeology, anthropology, geology, botany and zoology.

Kyoto National Museum, Japan

www.kyohaku.go.jp

Japanese and Eastern Asian works of art and archaeological artefacts are housed by this museum. The website also has an impressive collection of East Asian images on the internet and a special section for children. See also the Tokyo National Museum at www.tnm.go.jp.

London Canal Museum

www.canalmuseum.org.uk

On this website you can find out the history of London's canals, the cargoes carried, the people who lived and worked on the waterways, and the horses that pulled their boats. It provides useful educational resources.

London Transport Museum

www.ltmuseum.co.uk

This website helps to conserve and explain the capital city's transport heritage whilst engaging people in the debate about its future. The London Transport Museum has an extensive and attractve online presence and there is much more than just visitor information here.

Museum in Docklands

www.museumindocklands.org.uk

The Museum in Docklands, situated in the heart of London's docklands, explores the 2,000 year history of London's river, port and people, from the earliest settlements through to the recent regeneration of the former docklands. The museum offers extensive educational services for schools.

Museum of Garden History

www.museumgardenhistory.org

The aim of the museum, which is next to Lambeth Palace in London, is to illustrate and preserve the history of gardening. The museum has an extensive online presence, with images and detailed descriptions and includes a virtual tour.

Museum of London

www.museumoflondon.org.uk

Representing a quarter of a million years of history and over seven million Londoners, the Museum of London's collection includes over a million items. The museum has a huge online presence with many fascinating features.

Museum Stuff

www.museumstuff.com

A leading gateway to museums around the world but focusing mainly on US institutions with links to online educational and entertaining material.

Museums and Galleries

www.123world.com/ museumsandgalleries

A gateway to online museums and galleries across the world, organised in alphabetical order. The website has links to The Louvre, France and the Museo del Prado, Spain.

Museums of Britain

www.information-museums.co.uk

This online guide to over 1,000 museums across the UK, with descriptions and useful visitor information, is easily navigated by county or type.

Museums on the Web

www.mda.org.uk/vlmp

An extremely useful portal with an alphabetical list of UK museum websites plus descriptions for easy reference. There is extensive coverage from the Aerospace Museum to The York Dungeon.

National Army Museum

www.national-army-museum.ac.uk

A fascinating museum, situated in central London, that tells the story of the British Army from Agincourt in the fifteenth century to peace-keeping in the twenty-first century.

National Maritime Museum

www.nmm.ac.uk

The National Maritime Museum and the Royal Observatory Greenwich are together on one website. Inspiring material about the sea, ships, time and the stars and the impact they have had on our lives are all here.

National Railway Museum

www.nrm.org.uk

The National Railway Museum based at York, is considered the largest railway museum in the world. Its website is part of the National Grid for Learning and contains excellent educational resources for all ages and levels.

Natural History Museum

www.nhm.ac.uk

One of the world's most famous museums, the NHM in London was the first UK museum with an online presence (in 1994). Their attractive website has oodles of educational material. It is the UK's national museum of nature and a centre of scientific excellence.

Old Operating Theatre

www.thegarret.org.uk

A fascinating and chilling exploration of the reality of medicine and operations in the days before anaesthetics and antiseptic surgery. There are enthralling educational resources here on this website including virtual tours of the UK's oldest operating theatre and of St Thomas Hospital.

Petrie Museum of Egyptian Archaeology

www.petrie.ucl.ac.uk

The Petrie Museum is based at University College London. They have a growing range of teaching resources for different ages and abilities.

RAF Museum

www.rafmuseum.org.uk

The website of the RAF's two museums at Hendon in North London and Cosford in Shropshire. The website includes great images and extensive aviation history resources.

Science Museum

www.sciencemuseum.org.uk

One of London's best-known museums. It is educational, informative, inspiring and entertaining with lots of interactive science here too. The collections form a record of scientific, technological and medical change since the eighteenth century.

Smithsonian Institution

www.si.edu

With 17 museums and 140 affiliate museums, the world-famous Smithsonian Institution showcases US history, heritage and identity and promotes innovation, research and science. It is an inspiring online presence.

State Hermitage Museum

www.hermitagemuseum.org

One of the world's most famous museums, the Hermitage in St Petersburg, Russia, was put together over 250 years. Its collection of over 3 million works presents the development of world culture and art

M 131

from the Stone Age to the twenty-first century. The museum's excellent online presence includes a virtual visit, virtual viewings and virtual academy.

Thackray Museum

www.thackraymuseum.org

The Thackray Museum in Leeds has displays which explain how people's lives have changed over the last 150 years as a result of improvements in public health, medicine and healthcare.

Uffizi Gallery

www.polomuseale.firenze.it/english /uffizi

The Uffizi gallery in Florence (Firenze) is home to some of the world's most famous renaissance works of art, including those by Michaelangelo, Botticelli and Canaletto.

Vatican

http://mv.vatican.va

On the Vatican website you can take virtual tours around the Vatican Museums including the Sistine Chapel and Raphael's Rooms or view selected works such as Leonardo da Vinci's St Jerome.

Victoria and Albert Museum

www.vam.ac.uk

One of the world's most famous museums, the V and A in London has inspired and informed visitors for over 150 years with its mammoth collection of applied and decorative arts. The V and A's website includes lots of learning resources.

Virtual Library Museums Pages

www.icom.museum/vlmp

A useful directory of online museums and museum-related resources.

Music

There is a vast amount of information here, covering all tastes and styles and every aspect of this important subject. This category includes festivals, the history of music, individual music tuition, exam papers, lessons online, seats of learning, advice on purchasing instruments, music guides, sound effects, composers' biographies, MP3s, and much more. This category will keep your mind and ears spinning!

African Music Encyclopedia

All About Jazz

All Music Guide

Artist Direct

Associated Board of the Royal Schools
   of Music

BBC Music

BBC Top of the Pops

BRIT Awards

British Academy of Composers and
   Songwriters

British Phonographic Industry

British Underground Rock Bands

Brtitish Music Information Centre

ChoralNet

Classical Composers Database

Classical Digest

Classical Music Archives

Classical Music Pages

ClassicalLink

ClassicalNet

Click Music

English National Opera

Find Me the Sound

Folk Archive Resource North East

GMN Arts Network

GRAMMY

Handel House Museum

Hobgoblin Music

I'm Gifted

Jazz Online

Lyrics

Music Education Council

Musical Resources

MusicAtSchool

MusicBizBuzz

Musicians' Union

M 134

MusicLand

MusicTeachers

My Music Index

National Anthems

National Youth Orchestra

Naxos

OrchestraNET

Pay The Piper

Performing Rights Society

Popworld

Reggae Train

Royal Academy of Music

Royal College of Music

Royal Opera House

Soul City Limits

Sounddogs

Synth Zone

This Day In Music

Vitaminic

Vocalist

Youth Music

Music – Instruments

ABC Music

All Flutes Plus

Allodi Accordions

Andy's Guitars

BEM Music

Bina Musical Stores

Blanks Music Stores

Bridgewood and Neitzert

Chandler Guitars

Chappell of Bond Street

Chimes Music

Ealing Strings

Foote's

Gallery Bass Merchant

Holywell Music

Ivor Mairants Musicentre

J & A Beare

London Guitar Studio

Macari's

Markson Pianos

Music Ground

Musical Instrument Sales

Musicnotes

Phil Parker Ltd

Portobello Music

Pro Percussion

Spanish Guitar Centre

Steinway and Sons

TW Howarth

Vintage and Rare Guitars

Wembley Drum Centre

World of Music

Music – Lessons

BBC Music – Learning an Instrument

Britchops Drum Tuition

Classic Guitar Instruction

Fluteland

Guitar Tab Universe

Hornplayer

Online Guitar Archive

Riff Interactive

Songplayer

Violin Online

African Music Encyclopedia

www.africanmusic.org

This website has links, information and biographies about African music and musicians.

All About Jazz

www.allaboutjazz.com

A comprehensive and entertaining site for jazz fans. It includes news, interviews, reviews, profiles and a global jazz guide.

All Music Guide

www.allmusic.com

This guide is a veritable goldmine of information about music, artists and bands, covering every genre. It is US oriented but has lots of UK material.

Associated Board of the Royal Schools of Music

www.abrsm.ac.uk

Details of ABRSM exams and a useful FAQ section are available on this website. You can find out about the fees for each grade, examination papers, advice for pupils, parents and teachers. An invaluable site for those taking music exams.

BBC Music

www.bbc.co.uk/music

The BBC's excellent and comprehensive music site includes news, reviews and listings covering every kind of music.

BBC Top of the Pops

www.bbc.co.uk/totp

The official TOTP website, updated twice a day 7 days a week with the latest pop news, features, interviews, gossip and loads of information.

BRIT Awards

www.brits.co.uk

A website all about the annual BRIT awards, but it is updated throughout the year with news, competitions, photos and a messageboard.

British Academy of Composers and Songwriters

www.britishacademy.com

This website provides information and advice for aspiring songwriters and composers from the association that represents the UK's songwriting and composing community.

British Phonographic Industry

www.bpi.co.uk

'Promoting and protecting British music', the BPI is the trade association for the UK record industry, representing British

M 135

record companies from the largest corporation to the smallest label. Their work includes dealing with music piracy and managing the official UK charts.

British Underground Rock Bands

www.burbs.co.uk

An excellent guide to independent – or unsigned – rock bands from around the UK. It has all the latest news and gig guides, streaming audio and links to individual band sites.

Brtitish Music Information Centre

www.bmic.co.uk

A good resource for people interested in British music from the twentieth and twenty-first Century. The website contains collections, links, events, news and features.

ChoralNet

www.choralnet.org

Providing a portal for the worldwide choral community, ChoralNet includes a variety of mailing lists, forums, links to choral organisations and choirs, plus extensive reference material and more. An extremely useful resource for music students and teachers.

Classical Composers Database

www.classical-composers.org

The detailed information about composers is continuously updated and the site welcomes contributions.

Classical Digest

www.classicaldigest.com

Classical Digest claims to be the world's largest review reference base for classical music on CD and DVD.

Classical Music Archives

www.classicalarchives.com

A US site that claims to be the largest classical music archive on the net. You can listen to sections of your favourite composers' works here or subscribe to receive more extensive material.

Classical Music Pages

http://w3.rz-berlin.mpg.de/cmp

An extensive classical music resource. Its history, biographical information about composers, explanations of musical forms and a dictionary of musical terminology is of use to both beginners and professionals.

ClassicalLink

www.classicallink.com

A portal site that provides visitors with access to a large number of websites which are all selected for their focus on classical and related music.

ClassicalNet

www.classical.net

ClassicalNet has over 3,000 CD, DVD and book reviews plus 6,000 files and 4,000 links to other classical music sites.

Click Music

www.clickmusic.co.uk

A music search engine where you can search for music websites or bands, check for the latest music reviews and for information about musical events.

English National Opera

www.eno.org

This website has extensive information on the professional world of opera in the UK. You can visit the educational projects run by this famous institution and explore the features and history of opera.

Find Me the Sound

www.findmethesound.com

A music portal to find musicians, ensembles, groups, suppliers, agencies, live music and festivals.

Folk Archive Resource North East

www.asaplive.com/farne/home.cfm

Welcome to FARNE, home of Northumbrian music online. From here you can access 4,000 songs, tunes, sound recordings and photographs from across the North East of England, bringing the musical heritage of the region alive.

GMN Arts Network

www.gmn.com

The latest news from around the globe is available on this website covering classical music, jazz, opera and world music. It has an extensive range of content online, including audio and video, MP3 downloads, interviews, features, radio, forums and shopping.

GRAMMY

www.grammy.com

The GRAMMY awards are presented to honour excellence in the recording arts and sciences, and are awarded by artists to artists. There are lots of news and features from the music industry here too plus intelligent reviews and stories. This is a site for the serious music fan.

Handel House Museum

www.handelhouse.org

This house belonged to the famous musician George Friederic Handel from 1723 until his death in 1759.

Hobgoblin Music

www.hobgoblin.com

Hobgoblin Music provide extensive information and advice about folk, traditional and Celtic music. The website includes an events guide plus instrument advice and sales.

I'm Gifted

www.imgifted.co.uk

Do you want to be a pop star? On this website you will find advice on making your first recording, promoting yourself, marketing and information about the pop business.

Jazz Online

www.jazzonline.com

A great online, interactive magazine covering all styles of jazz music, this site is a must for jazz fans.

M 137

Lyrics

www.lyrics.com

The lyrics of hundreds of songs from well-known artists are all organised alphabetically on this website.

Music Education Council

www.mec.org.uk

The Music Education Council promotes and supports all aspects of music education in the UK and raises public awareness of its purpose and benefits. This website has good links for pupils and teachers too.

Musical Resources

www.musicalresources.co.uk

A-level resources, compositions, concert reviews, links, forums and more are all available on this website.

MusicAtSchool

www.musicatschool.co.uk

MusicAtSchool provides resources, internet links, free worksheets, quizzes, online lessons and homework help for secondary school music students and teachers.

MusicBizBuzz

www.musicbizbuzz.net

A huge US-oriented directory site covering anything and everything to do with the music business worldwide.

Musicians' Union

www.musiciansunion.org.uk

The Musicians' Union promotes and protects the interests of musicians across the UK. Their website gives details of the Union's work and services for musicians.

MusicLand

www.themusicland.co.uk

The UK's portal and online community for music education with academic resources for teachers and pupils. You will need to register to gain access to the site's information.

MusicTeachers

www.musicteachers.co.uk

On this website you can find a music teacher anywhere in the UK. Plus it has links to theory papers, aural tests and other resources for pupils studying music.

My Music Index

www.mymusicindex.com

This is a quick reference informational music resource which is useful for both educators and students and consists of a collection of musical links.

National Anthems

www.national-anthems.org

A website containing national anthems from around the world. It has detailed information, with sheet music and texts to download and purchase.

National Youth Orchestra

www.nyo.org.uk

The NYO is one of the world's finest youth orchestras and draws together over 150 talented musicians from across the UK, aged 13 to 19. Details on how to audition are available on this website.

Naxos

www.naxos.com

The learning zone of the Naxos site includes useful material for music students, including A to Zs of opera and classical music plus extensive links.

OrchestraNET

www.orchestranet.co.uk

OrchestraNET has links to orchestras, live works, books and all things orchestral.

Pay The Piper

www.paythepiper.co.uk

A guide to choosing what instrument to play, advice on how to buy an instrument, where to get practice, finding opportunities to play, tackling music exams and much more.

Performing Rights Society

www.prs.co.uk

All about the work of the PRS, which collects licence fees for the public performance and broadcast of musical works and distributes the money to writers and publishers.

Popworld

www.popworld.com

Popworld claims to be the 'biggest and best' pop website in the world. The website has the hottest news and gossip, the latest reviews, the best features and the biggest stars.

Reggae Train

www.reggaetrain.com

This website claims to be the largest and most comprehensive reggae music portal site on the internet. It is a huge resource for all reggae fans.

Royal Academy of Music

www.ram.ac.uk

The Royal Academy of Music is one of the leading institutions for musical education in the world and features programmes for juniors as well as older students and pupils. If you are interested in becoming a musician then this website will be of great interest.

Royal College of Music

www.rcm.ac.uk

The Royal College of Music is one of the world's leading musical institutions, providing musical education and training at the highest international level for musicians, singers and composers.

Royal Opera House

www.royaloperahouse.org

On the Royal Opera House's website you can view ticket availability for current performances and learn more about the history of the Opera House plus find out what is on offer from this prestigious institution.

Soul City Limits

www.soulcitylimits.com

A website for soul music fans. It covers all forms of soul.

Sounddogs

www.sounddogs.com

A sound effects library on the internet, with over 200,000 sounds.

Synth Zone

www.synthzone.com

A useful resource for anyone interested in synth music. It has extensive links, reviews of gadgets, instruments and software and a regular newsletter with updates.

This Day In Music

www.thisdayinmusic.com

This website can tell you what happened in the world of music on a particular day in previous years. Plus it has a whole heap of other music trivia.

Artist Direct

www.artistdirect.com

A massive portal site with links to all sorts of music information available on the internet. You can search for artists, bands, concerts, venues, record labels, festivals, online music magazines and much more.

Vitaminic

www.vitaminic.co.uk

Discover on this website new musicians who have chosen to put their music out on the internet in MP3 format. A directory, categorised by genre, with information about each artist/band and links so that you can listen to their music.

Vocalist

www.vocalist.org.uk

Do you want to be a singer? This site is dedicated to singers, vocalists, singing teachers and students of all ages, styles and standards. It is a comprehensive resource with stacks of information on all aspects of singing.

Youth Music

www.youthmusic.org.uk

Youth Music is a national charity that provides high quality and diverse music-making for children up to age 18, targeting young people in areas of social and economic need who may otherwise lack the opportunity to engage in music.

Music – Instruments

ABC Music

www.abcmusic.co.uk

A general and sheet music website.

All Flutes Plus

www.allflutesplus.co.uk

A website all about flutes.

Allodi Accordions

www.accordions.co.uk

A website all about accordions.

Andy's Guitars

www.andysguitarnet.com

A website all about guitars.

BEM Music

www.bem-music.com

A website all about guitars and keyboards.

Bina Musical Stores

www.binaswar.com

A general music website.

Blanks Music Stores

www.blanksmusic.co.uk

A general music website.

Bridgewood and Neitzert

www.londonviolins.com

A website all about violins.

Chandler Guitars

www.chandlerguitars.co.uk

A website all about guitars.

Chappell of Bond Street

www.chappellofbondstreet.co.uk

A general and sheet music website.

Chimes Music

www.chimesmusic.com

A general and sheet music website.

Ealing Strings

www.ealingstrings.info

A website all about string instruments.

Foote's

www.footesmusic.com

A website all about drums, percussion, woodwind, brass and string instruments.

Gallery Bass Merchant

www.thebassgallery.com

A website all about bass guitars.

Holywell Music

www.holywellmusic.com

A website all about harps.

Ivor Mairants Musicentre

www.ivormairants.co.uk

A website all about guitars.

J & A Beare

www.beares.com

A website all about strings.

London Guitar Studio

www.londonguitarstudio.com

A website all about guitars.

Macari's

www.macaris.co.uk

A website all about guitars and brass instruments.

Markson Pianos

www.pianosuk.co.uk

A website of the leading UK piano specialists

Music Ground

www.musicground.com

A website all about guitars.

Musical Instrument Sales

www.musicalinstrumentsales.co.uk

A general music website.

Musicnotes

www.musicnotes.com

A website on sheet music.

Phil Parker Ltd

www.philparker.co.uk

A website all about brass instruments.

Portobello Music

www.fiddles.demon.co.uk

A website all about guitars and string instruments.

Pro Percussion

www.propercussion.co.uk

A website all about percussion instruments.

Spanish Guitar Centre

www.spanishguitarcentre.com

A website all about Spanish guitars.

Steinway and Sons

www.steinway.com

A website all about pianos.

TW Howarth

www.howarth.uk.com

A website all about woodwind instruments.

Vintage and Rare Guitars

www.vintageandrareguitars.com

A website on vintage and rare guitars.

Wembley Drum Centre

www.wembleydrumcentre.com

A website all about drums.

World of Music

www.wom.co.uk

This website covers guitars and pianos.

Music – Lessons

BBC Music – Learning an Instrument

www.bbc.co.uk/music/parents/ learninganinstrument

Lessons in general music are available from this website.

Britchops Drum Tuition

www.britchops.co.uk

Drum lessons are availabel from this website.

Classic Guitar Instruction

www.classic-guitar.com

Guitar lessons are available from this website.

Fluteland

www.fluteland.com

Flute lessons are available from this website.

Guitar Tab Universe

www.guitartabs.cc/home.php

Guitar lessons are available from this website.

Hornplayer

www.hornplayer.net

French Horn lessons are available from this website.

Online Guitar Archive

www.olga.net

Guitar lessons are available from this website.

Riff Interactive

www.riffinteractive.com

Guitar lessons are available from this website.

Songplayer

www.songplayer.com

Guitar and keyboard lessons are available from this website.

Violin Online

www.violinonline.com

Violin lessons are available from this website.

Parents and Guardians

From children's homework to information on choosing a school, the sites listed here include advice for safe surfing on the internet, parents' information networks, parents and teachers associations plus numerous other resources. **You may find that the other individual categories in this book will also hold useful information, depending on the age, ability and interests of the children you care for. The Education and Teachers category also holds beneficial educational links.**

Advisory Centre for Education

All 4 Kids

All Kids

BBC Parents' Music Room

Boarding Schools Association

Chatdanger

Child Alert

Childcare Link

Childnet International

Childrens Money World

Daycare Trust

Emetis – Independent Schools Advice

Families Need Fathers

ForParentsByParents

Gingerbread

Incorporated Association of Preparatory Schools

Independent Schools Council

Internet Content Rating Association

Just Ask

Kidscape

Kids-Party

Learning and Skills Council

Missing Children

National Children's Bureau

National Confederation of Parent Teacher Associations

Natural Parenting UK

NCH – the Children's Charity

Office for Standards in Education

One Parent Families

Parent Centre

Parentline Plus

Parents Information Network

Parents Centre

ParentsTalk

Project Happy Child

Raising Kids

Safe Kids

Safe Teens

Secondary Schools Online

Smartparent

Trust for the Study of Adolescence

UK Boarding School Search

UK Parents

UK Self Help

Advisory Centre for Education

www.ace-ed.org.uk

ACE is an independent advice centre for parents, offering information about state education in England and Wales for 5–16 year olds. They provide advice on topics such as exclusion from school, bullying, special needs and school admission appeals.

All 4 Kids

www.all4kidsuk.com

A helpful site with lots of useful information about local, regional and national organisations and individuals offering products and services specifically for children and their families.

All Kids

www.allkids.co.uk

An online parenting magazine with heaps of material. The website includes sections on shopping for kids, a parents' information directory and free fun sites for children.

BBC Parents' Music Room

www.bbc.co.uk/music/parents

This is a website for parents who want to develop, motivate and support their childrens' musical talent. It is good for music teachers too and contains useful advice and information on music.

Boarding Schools Association

www.boarding.org.uk

The BSA offers a consultancy service to parents and young people considering a boarding education as well as a directory of boarding schools and a range of other services.

Chatdanger

www.chatdanger.com

An excellent site that highlights the dangers of online chatrooms and guides parents about how to keep their children safe. It is a good parents' guide and provides an interesting overview of the internet and what it has to offer for children and families.

Child Alert

www.childalert.co.uk

Advice, information, links and products to help parents and guardians bring up children in a safe environment are all available on this website.

Childcare Link

www.childcarelink.gov.uk

Childcare Link provide help with finding useful information about childcare and early education facilities and services in your local area.

Childnet International

www.childnet-int.org

Taking a balanced approach to the internet, while responding to the negative aspects and dangers for children, Childnet's website promotes the positive and highlights the inspirational and creative ways in which children are using the internet as a force for good.

Childrens Money World

www.childrensmoneyworld.com

This website provides software for teaching children mathematics and numeracy using money and finance, thus helping to develop money management at an early age.

Daycare Trust

www.daycaretrust.org.uk

The Daycare Trust works to promote access to quality, affordable childcare for all who need it.

Emetis – Independent Schools Advice

www.emetis.com

Emetis provide information about UK independent schools, boarding schools and day schools. On their website you can learn more about the UK education system, search for schools or download helpful e-books and documents.

Families Need Fathers

www.fnf.org.uk

FNF believes that, in the event of a family breakdown, children have a right to a continuing loving relationship with both parents and need to be protected from the harm of losing contact with one parent.

ForParentsByParents

www.forparentsbyparents.com

Funded, founded and maintained by parents, this site aims to give an honest view of parenting and to reflect the reality of being a parent. It also includes useful sections on shopping for children, entertaining them, family holidays and much more.

Gingerbread

www.gingerbread.org.uk

Gingerbread provides valuable information, support and advice for lone parent families in the UK.

Incorporated Association of Preparatory Schools

www.iaps.org.uk

This website has information for parents, pupils, governors and teachers about education in preparatory schools, plus details of the services provided by IAPS which is the Association of Heads of Preparatory Schools.

Independent Schools Council

www.isis.org.uk

A website that enables parents to check through the 1,300 schools accredited to the ISC, helping to choose the right school for their child. It is an authoritative starting point when searching for an independent school.

Internet Content Rating Association

www.icra.org/about

An independent organisation that rates websites and measures the content for suitability for children. They aim to protect children from potentially harmful material while protecting free speech on the internet.

Just Ask

www.justask.org.uk

Just Ask is the first place to ask about legal help and information in England and Wales from the Community Legal Service.

Kidscape

www.kidscape.org.uk

Kidscape is a national charity dedicated to preventing bullying and child abuse. It provides individuals and organisations with the skills and resources required to keep children safe.

Kids-Party

www.kids-party.com

This website has tips and advice about organising children's parties. It also has pointers to handy places where you can buy gifts or party accessories and also advises about party services such as comedians or film crews.

Learning and Skills Council

www.lsc.gov.uk

The Learning and Skills Council is responsible for funding and planning all post-16 education and training in England, other than at universities.

Missing Children

www.missingkids.co.uk

A site dedicated to helping reunite children with their families. It offers advice and resources for parents and anybody who may want to help with useful information.

National Children's Bureau

www.ncb.org.uk

The NCB promotes the interests and well-being of children and young people, and advocates the participation of children and young people in all matters affecting them.

National Confederation of Parent Teacher Associations

www.ncpta.org.uk

The NCPTA promotes effective partnerships between parents and teachers in order to foster learning opportunities at school and at home.

Natural Parenting UK

www.natural-parenting.com

A natural parenting information and resources website which covers everything from pregnancy and birth through to feeding, sleeping, health and education.

NCH – the Children's Charity

www.nchafc.org.uk

NCH helps children at risk or in care, vulnerable young people and families under pressure. Their work covers adoption, disability, early years, family support, education, family placement, health, participation, family rights, residential care and youth services.

Office for Standards in Education

www.ofsted.gov.uk

The work of Ofsted, whose main aim is to help improve the quality and standards of education and childcare through independent inspection and regulation.

One Parent Families

www.oneparentfamilies.org.uk

One Parent Families promotes the welfare of lone parents and their children. The organisation's aim is to overcome the poverty, isolation and social exclusion which many lone parents face. Their website has lots of useful information and advice.

Parent Centre

www.parentcentre.gov.uk

An attractive and easy-to-use website from the DfES which acts as a reference book for the education system and a guide to sources of further information. The website is split into age groups and it also includes sections on choosing a school, what your child learns, school life, rights, responsibilities and special needs.

Parentline Plus

www.parentlineplus.org.uk

Parentline Plus offer support to anyone parenting a child. Help is available here for parents that find themselves in a difficult situation when dealing with their offspring.

Parents Information Network

www.pin.org.uk

PIN provides guidance on computers and education for parents with children from toddlers up to 18 years old. The website also provides excellent guidance on how parents can evaluate the suitability of both software and websites.

Parents Centre

www.parentscentre.gov.uk

This website aims to help families to make the most of the internet and provides information on how to use it safely. Parents Online has been created by the DfES to promote home-school links by helping parents understand the role of ICT in learning.

ParentsTalk

www.parents-talk.com

An online magazine with parenting tips, activities for families, links to fun sites for kids, crafts for children, and a range of information for parents. The website also has parenting advice from experts.

Project Happy Child

www.happychild.org.uk

An index of resources, events, directories, free educational resources, special needs resources, charities and more for parents, teachers and children.

Raising Kids

www.raisingkids.co.uk

Raising Kids has more than 1,000 webpages filled with helpful advice about being a parent which are split into neat child age and topic categories. The site also includes online competitions, features and discussion boards for parents and the latest developments in education.

Safe Kids

www.safekids.com

Chatroom and internet safety are just two of the safety issues explained on this US site. It also has a collection of features explaining what net safety is about and how to cope with any problems that may arise.

Safe Teens

www.safeteens.com

Safe Teens has plenty of good advice on net safety and net manners for teenagers and their parents. Safe Teens is from the same people who manage www.safekids.com.

Secondary Schools Online

www.secondaryschoolsonline. co.uk

A simple alphabetical directory with links to websites of secondary schools across England.

Smartparent

www.smartparent.com

This US site's aim is to educate parents on how to safeguard children in cyberspace. There is information on blocking and filtering software, tips on protection and links to parent/child friendly sites. Their goal is to help keep childrens' online experiences safe, educational and entertaining.

Trust for the Study of Adolescence

www.tsa.uk.com

TSA is a research, training and development organisation that aims to improve the lives of young people, and their families, through improving knowledge and understanding about adolescence and young adulthood.

UK Boarding School Search

www.darch.co.uk

A comprehensive listing of UK boarding schools, both primary and secondary. You can search by name, location, type of school or look for schools that offer particular facilities.

UK Parents

www.ukparents.co.uk

Exchange real life experiences with other parents on this website. There are loads of resources at this online community for new and not so new parents. Information, entertainment, help, support and friendship are all provided on one site.

UK Self Help

www.ukselfhelp.info

UK Self Help is an excellent source of information and assistance. It has a directory of over 800 UK self help groups listed in alphabetical order by subject covering everything from abducted children to the XXY Syndrome.

Politics

Political parties, special interest groups and civil society organisations maintain a website to spread the word and promote their causes. Here you can keep up with the latest policies and campaigns, find out about European legislation or follow the work of human rights groups and you can give your views and opinions too. **The resources here complement some of the sites listed in the Social Sciences and History categories and should help you to broaden your knowledge.**

10 Downing Street

Adam Smith Institute

Amnesty International

BBC Politics

British Monarchy

Commonwealth Secretariat

Conservative Party

DirectGov

ePolitix

Europa

European Youth Parliament

eXplore Parliament

Fax Your MP

Foreign and Commonwealth Office

Green Party

Guardian Unlimited – Politics

HeadsUp

Human Rights Watch

Labour Party

Liberal Democrats

Liberty

National Assembly for Wales

People and Politics

Plaid Cymru

Political Resources on the Net

Political Studies Association

Royal Institute of International Affairs

Scottish National Party

Scottish Parliament

Sinn Fein

Trades Union Congress

UK Independence Party

UK Office of the European Parliament

UK Parliament

UK Politics Directory

UK Youth Parliament

Ulster Unionist Party

United Nations

Voices of Youth

Westminster Watch

White House

Working Paper Sites of Political
Science

Worldaware

Young Commonwealth

10 Downing Street

www.number-10.gov.uk

The British Prime Minister's comprehensive official website with news, speeches, briefings, announcements and much more. The website also includes an excellent historical section, with a photogallery and a tour of the PM's office and residence.

Adam Smith Institute

www.adamsmith.org

The website of the influential economic policy institute that promotes the principles of free markets and a free society.

Amnesty International

www.amnesty.org

The official website of the worldwide movement that campaigns for human rights. Their website has detailed – and sometimes distressing – information about the people and causes it champions, plus advice about how you can support their work.

BBC Politics

www.bbc.co.uk/politics

All of the latest news from the world of politics is on this website.

British Monarchy

www.royal.gov.uk

The official site for the Monarchy, covering the Monarchy today, the Royal Family, the history of the Monarchy and information about the royal residences and artwork.

Commonwealth Secretariat

www.thecommonwealth.org

The Commonwealth Secretariat implements the decisions taken by the 53 member governments of the Commonwealth. Their website gives information on member countries, activities and projects.

Conservative Party

www.conservatives.com

The official website of the Conservative Party.

DirectGov

www.direct.gov.uk

A guide to government information and services available online. The website includes updated information from hundreds of other government sites.

P 151

ePolitix

www.epolitix.com

A comprehensive site that aims to 'improve communication between elected representatives and the public'. It has extensive news coverage, features, forum and a big collection of MP's websites.

Europa

www.europa.eu.int

The portal site of the European Union, Europa provides coverage of EU affairs and information about European integration issues.

European Youth Parliament

www.eyp.org/intro.htm

Founded in 1987, the EYP seeks to promote the European dimension in education and give students aged 16 to 22 an increased awareness of European issues. The EYP experience 'encourages young people to be aware of the thoughts and characteristics of other nations, respect their differences and learn to work together for a common good.'

eXplore Parliament

www.explore.parliament.uk

Designed for young people, eXplore Parliament is an attractive, friendly, interactive website that explains how parliament works. It includes a useful teachers' centre.

Fax Your MP

www.faxyourmp.com

This website provides the easy way to write to your MP. You just use the interactive form available on this independently run site and, if you don't know who your MP is, you can just type in your postcode to find out.

Foreign and Commonwealth Office

www.fco.gov.uk

The UK's foreign policy is explained on this website, along with information about careers in the Foreign Office, travel advice for every country in the world and links to UK Embassies overseas.

Green Party

www.greenparty.org.uk

Political issues from an environmental perspective on the Green Party's website.

Guardian Unlimited – Politics

www.politics.guardian.co.uk

The political pages of Guardian Unlimited provide much more than daily political news and comment. A huge and well organised resource, with many excellent articles and special reports, plus extensive links.

HeadsUp

www.headsup.org.uk

Run by The Hansard Society, an independent education charity, HeadsUp encourages young people to engage in politics and provides a safe forum for under 18s to discuss their political views with MPs and other young people.

Human Rights Watch

www.hrw.org

The website of the independent non-governmental organisation dedicated to protecting the human rights of people around the world.

Labour Party

www.labour.org.uk

The official website of the Labour Party.

Liberal Democrats

www.libdems.org.uk

The official website of the Liberal Democrats.

Liberty

www.liberty-human-rights.org.uk

The website of the leading UK civil liberties and human rights campaigning group, Liberty.

National Assembly for Wales

www.wales.gov.uk

This website contains the work of the National Assembly for Wales and the Welsh Assembly Government.

People and Politics

www.political.org.uk

A simple portal site that provides an index of who's who in UK politics.

Plaid Cymru

www.plaidcymru.org

The official website of Plaid Cymru (The Party of Wales).

Political Resources on the Net

www.politicalresources.net

An extensive directory of political sites from around the world, with links to parties, governments, the media and other organizations.

Political Studies Association

www.psa.ac.uk

The aim of the Association is to promote and develop the study of politics. Their website includes information about the Association's work, publications and details of events.

Royal Institute of International Affairs

www.riia.org

The RIIA is one of the world's leading institutes for the analysis of international issues. Their website contains details of their meetings, conferences, research and publications.

Scottish National Party

www.snp.org.uk

The official website of the Scottish National Party.

Scottish Parliament

www.scottish.parliament.uk

This website is all about the work of the Scottish Parliament.

Sinn Fein

www.sinnfein.ie

The official website of Sinn Fein.

Trades Union Congress

www.tuc.org.uk

The TUC is the umbrella organisation for the trade union movement in the UK, representing over seven million working people.

UK Independence Party

www.independenceuk.org.uk

The official website of the UK Independence Party.

UK Office of the European Parliament

www.europarl.org.uk

The website of the UK Office of the European Parliament. It includes details of the Parliament's work and information about the UK's MEPs.

UK Parliament

www.parliament.uk

An attractive site with well-presented, detailed information about the workings of the Houses of Parliament.

UK Politics Directory

www.uk-p.org

A directory of nearly 2,000 links to a wide range of political websites such as parties, organisations and government departments.

UK Youth Parliament

www.ukyouthparliament.org.uk

The Youth Parliament gives the young people of the UK a voice which will be heard and listened to by local and national government, providers of services for young people and other agencies who have an interest in the views of young people. If you are aged between 11 and 18 you can vote for – or stand as – a MYP.

Ulster Unionist Party

www.uup.org

The official website of the Ulster Unionist Party.

United Nations

www.un.org

A mammoth website with comprehensive and detailed information about the work of the United Nations.

Voices of Youth

www.unicef.org/voy

Children across the world can have their say on current events, human rights and social issues on this site sponsored by UNICEF.

Westminster Watch

www.westminsterwatch.co.uk

Keeping an eye on politics, Westminster Watch is an easy to use magazine site devoted to political news, features, opinion and announcements.

White House

www.whitehouse.gov

All the latest news and announcements from The White House, the US President's office and home. There is a special section for young people and you can email The White House too.

Working Paper Sites of Political Science

www.workingpapers.org

A directory of links to the working papers of leading political scientists. This website is an excellent resource for serious students of politics.

Worldaware

www.worldaware.org.uk

Raising awareness of international development issues, Worldaware produces a range of resources for teachers and students in subjects such as geography, citizenship and sustainable development.

Young Commonwealth

www.youngcommonwealth.org

An attractive site explaining to young people what the Commonwealth is, what it does and which countries are members.

Reference and Revision

The sites in this category add value to the National Curriculum websites that are already included in the individual categories. It also provides invaluable support and advice for homework, revision, research, exams and general knowledge. Encyclopedias, coursework, quotations, libraries, Yellow Pages, National Curriculum Online and multiple reference resources on everyday topics and enquiries are provided here. **Further information can be sourced by visiting the individual category of your choice.**

192.com

Academic Database

Active Revision

Answer Bank

AS Guru

BBC Bitesize

BBC Learning

Biography

Brainy Quote

British Library

CGP Books

Consumer Complaints

Coursework Bank

Coursework.Info

Education Resources on the Internet

Encarta

Encyclopedia Britannica

Encyclopedia.com

Fact Monster

Floodlight

Free Dictionary

Free Library

HighBeam Research

HomeWork Elephant

How To Complain

HyperDictionary

Information Commissioner

Intellectual Property

Internet Public Library

KidsClick

Learning

Learning Alive

Learnthings

LibrarySpot

Living Library

Local Today

National Curriculum in Action

National Curriculum Online

Nobel e-Museum

Office of Fair Trading

Open Directory Project

PhotoLondon

Project GCSE

Public Record Office

Quotations Page

Revision Notes

Revisiontime

Rizer

SchoolsDirectory

Schoolzone

S-Cool

Sparknotes

Student Central

TagTeacherNet

TheBigProject

Tiscali Reference

Topmarks

UK Patent Office

Wikipedia

Xreferplus

Yell.com

192.com

www.192.com

A UK directory enquiry service that provides information on people, businesses, maps, addresses, products and services.

Academic Database

www.academicdb.com

Described as the Students' Academic Database this website houses more than 9,000 essays at university level across a broad range of subjects.

Active Revision

www.activerevision.com

From the publishers HarperCollins, this website provides help with resources for exams. The site recommends books on specific subjects that may help you to do better.

Answer Bank

www.theanswerbank.co.uk

The Answer Bank is a community question and answer site where users can ask genuine questions and receive helpful answers. It also provides a forum for debate on issues of general interest.

AS Guru

http:www.bbc.co.uk/education/ asguru

AS Guru provides a helping hand through your AS levels covering maths, English, biology and general studies.

BBC Bitesize

www.bbc.co.uk/schools/revision

This site from the BBC offers help with homework and revision. You can get help with school work by talking to people your own age, there is advice on revision techniques and dealing with school stress or you can simply take a break in the music and art rooms. This website is for all ages but primarily 7–16 year olds.

BBC Learning

www.bbc.co.uk/learning

BBC Learning provides educational resources for schools, colleges and higher education. There is a wealth of educational material here for all ages which is categorised under subject headings. On this website you will find courses, revision and study materials plus information and links on general topics for students.

Biography

www.biography.com

From William the Conqueror to Nelson Mandela and George Bush, you can find more than 25,000 biographies on the Biography website.

Brainy Quote

www.brainyquote.com

Brainy Quote has quotes by author, alphabetically organised by topic, plus famous quotes and, of course, the quote of the day.

British Library

www.bl.uk

The British Library's massive site has a digital library which is being updated all the time. Online visitors can read original manuscripts like the Magna Carta, browse through the Library's other treasures and click links to related subjects. The site is also home to the National Sound Archives, Churchill's speeches, Stravinsky rehearsing in 1948, sound effects and a whole

section with activities and resources for learning.

CGP Books

www.cpgbooks.co.uk

CGP Books have revision guides and study books for those exams!

Consumer Complaints

www.consumercomplaints.org.uk

This website is a free online service which allows you to make a consumer complaint to your local Trading Standards Service concerning any consumer problem you feel should be investigated.

Coursework Bank

www.courseworkbank.co.uk

A large database of coursework quality essays by students from 14 through to university level and covering a wide range of topics.

Coursework.Info

www.coursework.info

With over 63,000 essays and coursework, Coursework.Information offers a large academic database of information.

Education Resources on the Internet

www.edufind.com

An online service, operated by the Digital Education Network, which provides a range of internet based services for education. You can search for courses and services by country and category.

Encarta

www.encarta.msn.co.uk/reference

This website has snippets of wisdom from this very popular encyclopedia. The Encarta CD is also on sale here.

Encyclopedia Britannica

www.eb.com

The whole content of this comprehensive encyclopedia can be accessed now online for a subscription fee. One of the world's 'most trusted sources of information on every topic imaginable – from the origins of the Universe to current events and everything in between.'

Encyclopedia.com

www.encyclopedia.com

A great online encyclopedia. You can type in the topic and then read the answers or search by letter. There are detailed summaries, rather than pages of information, on just about everything.

Fact Monster

www.factmonster.com

Everyone will find something of interest on this entertaining site which has information on everything from the longest river, to traditions throughout the world. This site has all sorts of interesting facts and figures.

Floodlight

www.floodlight.co.uk

This is the official guide to courses in London. It covers full-time, part-time and evening courses run by government-funded colleges, universities and adult education centres in all of the London boroughs.

Free Dictionary

www.thefreedictionary.com

On this one site you will find English, medical, legal and computer dictionaries, a thesaurus, an encyclopedia, a literature reference library and a search engine.

Free Library

www.iln.net

Free Library is an online library with an extensive list of authors. For each author there is a biography, links to online texts and links to recommended websites. It is a sister site to Free Dictionary.

HighBeam Research

www.highbeam.com

A search facility with an archive of over 31 million documents from more than 2,700 sources. There is a collection of articles from leading publications which are updated daily and some date back up to 20 years. This website is ideal for research projects as it offers basic search results for free while full searches are available for a fee.

HomeWork Elephant

www.homeworkelephant.co.uk

This website offers help with homework. It has over 5,000 selected resources to help with homework problems and is divided by subject. Plus there are also hints and tips for parents and teachers.

How To Complain

www.howtocomplain.com

A useful complaining tool for when life treats you unfairly. This award winning site claims that more than 70 per cent of complaints logged here were resolved.

The content of this site is valid for the UK only.

HyperDictionary

www.hyperdictionary.com

HyperDictionary is not an ordinary dictionary. There are a choice of dictionaries on offer here. Type in a word in either the English dictionary, theasaurus, medical, or computer sections and you will find your response. Or you can try the dreams dictionary which explains the meanings of things appearing in your dreams.

Information Commissioner

www.informationcommissioner. gov.uk

The Information Commissioner's Office promotes good information handling practice and enforces data protection and freedom of information legislation. It encourages openness and accountability by the public services while championing respect for individual's private lives.

Intellectual Property

www.intellectual-property.gov.uk

A government site that aims to provide the resources needed to help you find your way through the intellectual property jungle of copyright, designs, patents and trade marks.

Internet Public Library

www.ipl.org

A uiversal internet resource with downloadable books, information and links on most subjects plus a special section with updates of news from around the world.

KidsClick

www.kidsclick.org

Research results tailored to suit young persons' needs, organised in a directory with more than 600+ subjects.

Learning

www.channel4.com/learning

The learning section of Channel 4's website provides students with some useful resources as well as a subscription area for GCSE's which has full access to a wide range of resources for applied GCSEs in ICT, business, science, health and social care and leisure and tourism.

Learning Alive

www.learningalive.co.uk

A useful homework resource for primary and secondary level students covering all subjects. There are subscription and free links to many select internet learning resources.

Learnthings

www.learn.co.uk

A curriculum based site from the Guardian newspaper, with top quality content which is divided into two sections. The site offers some free content while schools and registered members can also have access to further material from sister site, www.learnpremium.co.uk.

LibrarySpot

www.libraryspot.com

A free virtual library for all web explorers whether they are librarians, students or teachers. Encyclopedias on all subjects in the reference section are just a small part of the huge resources of information and directories available on this vast e-library resource.

Living Library

www.livinglibrary.co.uk

This homework resource is for primary and secondary school users. The information available comes with images from an extensive picture library. There are more than one million articles available through the Living Library with subjects relating to the national curriculum.

Local Today

www.localtoday.co.uk

Find out what's on in your area with this site where you can publicise your own event too.

National Curriculum in Action

www.ncaction.org.uk

Click on any subject of this resourceful site and find comments, examination papers and all you need to know about the national curriculum online. You can also view pupils comments as well as videos of them discussing different facets of the subject they are studying.

National Curriculum Online

www.nc.uk.net

Online resources covering every national curriculum subject. The website contains valuable information and is easy to navigate with a colourful design and layout.

Nobel e-Museum

www.nobel.se

The official website of the Nobel Foundation. The Nobel Prize is an international award, given yearly since 1901, for outstanding achievements in the areas of physics, chemistry, medicine, literature and peace. The website has information about all the winners (758 so far) plus the history of this prestigious award.

Office of Fair Trading

www.oft.gov.uk

Useful guidance from the website of the Office of Fair Trading, which aims to protect consumers, explain their rights and ensure that businesses operate and compete fairly.

Open Directory Project

www.dmoz.org

The Open Directory's aim is to become the definitive catalogue of the web. A huge, comprehensive human-edited directory, it is constructed and maintained by a global community of volunteer editors.

PhotoLondon

www.photolondon.org.uk

PhotoLondon is a superb photographic archive of London. The modern and historic photographs come from collections held by London's museums, libraries and archives.

Project GCSE

www.projectgcse.co.uk

Project GCSE provides resources for students revising for their GCSEs including revision notes and practice questions, a bookshop, help, advice and even a take a break section.

Public Record Office

www.pro.gov.uk

The UK's National Archive, which preserves government and law records going back to the eleventh century. It is a useful resource for genealogists and researchers.

Quotations Page

www.quotationspage.com

A veteran quotations site with thousands of quotations organised by subject or author.

Revision Notes

www.revision-notes.co.uk

Free revision notes and other resources for GCSE, A-Level, IB and university students to help with coursework and exams are all available from this website.

Revisiontime

www.revisiontime.com

An excellent free resource for students, teachers and parents with links to sites that are relevant to a broad category across the national curriculum of GCSE and A level subjects.

Rizer

www.rizer.co.uk

A government sponsored site with help on what to do if you are in trouble with the law. It offers information on how the criminal justice system works and the consequences of engaging in crime.

Schools Directory

www.schoolsdirectory.com

Schools Directory is a database of 33,000 primary, secondary, middle, independent and special needs schools across the UK. Each listing contains a full school description, the number on roll, Local Education Authority, Ofsted report, league tables, contact details and much more.

Schoolzone

www.schoolzone.co.uk

A search engine with recommended sites, homework help, advice for passing exams and what happens after finishing school.

S-Cool

www.s-cool.co.uk

The attractive S-Cool site contains excellent, informative and detailed revision notes covering all GCSE and A/AS-Level subjects, together with other useful information just for school students.

Sparknotes

www.sparknotes.com

Sparknotes has printable notes and study guides for students covering subjects like poetry, Shakespeare, literature and drama but also chemistry, biology and economics. You need to be a member to get more than the basics but it is free to join.

Student Central

www.studentcentral.co.uk

A collection of coursework and essays for GCSE, A-level and university. For the moment you can view samples of course work, submit your own and there is a facility to access the full content by paying a fee.

TagTeacherNet

www.tagteacher.net

A curriculum-referenced resource directory, teaching jobs, events directory, access to e-learning eligible products, key articles on education issues, making the most of IT in your classroom, newsletters plus more, and more.

TheBigProject

www.thebigproject.co.uk

A gateway to informative UK sites covering a wide range of subjects, from weather to joke of the day to translation services, links to reference websites and much more. See for yourself that there is something here for all interests.

Tiscali Reference

www.tiscali.co.uk/reference

This internet resource provider has dictionaries for plants, animals, English, computers plus information on health as well as directories and reference links.

Topmarks

www.topmarks.co.uk

A free directory maintained by teachers and listing the best resources on the web to help parents, students and teachers with the study of all national curriculum subjects.

UK Patent Office

www.patent.gov.uk

The Patent Office is responsible for intellectual property in the UK, which includes copyright, design, patents and trade marks.

Wikipedia

www.wikipedia.org

A free encyclopedia created by its online community users. It currently hosts 300,000 articles and encourages interested people to contribute with their own features and editing.

Xreferplus

www.xreferplus.com

This is an online database of 150+ encyclopedias and other reference resources. Xreferplus is an officially accredited digital learning resource for curriculum online. It is a multi-publisher reference service that offers access to over 157 titles taken from 36 of the 'names' in reference publishing with a user friendly subscription facility.

Yell.com

www.yell.co.uk

Yell.com is the Yellow Pages on the internet. Find what you are looking for here, whether it's a hairdresser or an Indian restaurant, a plumber or a stationer.

Science

This category includes physics, chemistry and biology with websites providing information on these subjects for the National Curriculum. It also includes the vast subject of space, supported by brilliant images, providing students, teachers and visitors of all ages with resources and links to help you research, explore, discover, enjoy – and attempt to understand – the universe.

S 164

21st Century

Annals of Improbable Research

Association for Science Education

Astronomy for Kids

Astronomy Now Online

BBC Gene Stories

BBC Science and Nature

Becoming Human

BioTopics

British National Space Centre

Cells Alive

Chemguide

Chemical Elements

Chemical Science Network

Creative Chemistry

Discover

Do Science

Earth and Sky

Echalk.co.uk

Experiments at School

Explore Mars Now

ExploreLearning

Extreme Science

Fun Science

Gemini Observatory

Gondar Design Science

How Stuff Works

Human Anatomy Online

Implosion World

Institute of Physics

Invention at Play

MadSci Network

Mark Rothery's Biology Web Site

NASA – National Aeronautics and Space Administration

Natural Hazards Education and Research Co-operative

New Scientist

Noise – New Outlooks in Science and
   Engineering

Physics.org

PhysicsWeb

Planet Science

RedNova

Royal Institution of Great Britain

Royal Observatory Greenwich

Royal Society

Schoolscience

Science Active

Science, Art and Human Perception

The Scientist

Scirus

Sodaplay

Space.com

SpaceDaily

SpaceWander

Students for the Exploration and
   Development of Space

Try Science

Volt Net

Web Elements

Windows to the Universe

Worldwide Web Journal of Biology

21st Century

www.21stcentury.co.uk

Attractive and absorbing, 21st Century is a
stylish science and technology news portal
that uses plain language to lead you
through often complex issues. This is a
must-visit site for those interested in new
technology and trends.

Annals of Improbable Research

www.improb.com

A humourous magazine filled with
improbable but genuine research drawn
from science, medicine and technology
journals. It is a good resource for science
teachers looking to intrigue and get
youngsters curious about science. The site
will make people laugh and then think.

Association for Science Education

www.ase.org.uk

ASE is the professional association
for teachers of science, though its
membership is open to others with an
interest in science teaching, including
students. The association publishes a
number of science journals and aims to
improve the teaching of science.

Astronomy for Kids

**www.frontiernet.net/~kidpower/
astronomy.html**

Astronomy for Kids provides
straightforward information for younger
students about the solar system, sun,
planets, stars, galaxies, asteroids, comets
and much more.

Astronomy Now Online

www.astronomynow.com

The website of the popular UK
astronomy magazine. It contains news
and views on space issues from a British
perspective.

BBC Gene Stories

www.bbc.co.uk/genes

The world of genes and how they shape our lives. This website is a great resource on genetics for teachers and students.

BBC Science and Nature

www.bbc.co.uk/science

Animals, prehistoric life, human body, mind, genes and space are just some of the interesting subjects covered in an entertaining way on this excellent BBC site.

Becoming Human

www.becominghuman.org

An entertaining, interactive 'documentary experience' detailing human evolution and development.

BioTopics

www.biotopics.co.uk

BioTopics has interactive educational material developed to help with biology study at secondary level.

British National Space Centre

www.bnsc.gov.uk

An excellent website from the BNSC, which co-ordinates the UK's civil space activity. You can learn all about the UK's space strategy, policy and future directions in space exploration. There are also some excellent links.

Cells Alive

www.cellsalive.com

An educational interactive website dedicated to the building blocks of life. The website includes cellular information in video clips and computer enhanced images.

Chemguide

www.chemguide.co.uk

A complete guide to chemistry for secondary level students up to A levels. Straight-forward and easy to browse through.

Chemical Elements

www.chemicalelements.com

An interactive periodic table of chemical elements.

Chemical Science Network

www.chemsoc.org

The visual elements periodic table is well designed with a striking visual impact. Other chemistry resources are also hosted by this site.

Creative Chemistry

www.creative-chemistry.org.uk

Chemistry activities, teaching notes and worksheets along with pages and pages with chemistry questions are on offer here for students and teachers of all levels.

Discover

www.discover.com

This online science magazine is user-friendly enough for non-scientists.

Do Science

www.doscience.com

A science site for students and teachers with experiments and activities that can be tried at home or at school.

Earth and Sky

www.earthsky.com

Science radio programmes discussing science subjects that have an impact on our everyday lives. Some shows focus on chemical processes in the earth's air and oceans while others take people on imaginary journeys into space exploring planets, the sun and a possible birth of a new solar system.

Echalk.co.uk

www.echalk.co.uk

This website is a free resource for teachers to use with interactive whiteboards and data projectors. An impressive and excellent tool for primary and secondary Science and Maths teachers using interactive whiteboards.

Experiments at School

www.experimentsatschool.org.uk

This data-handling website is aimed at getting students aged 7-19 across the UK to take part in statistics related experiments in five categories: life sciences, physical sciences, mathematics, geography and miscellaneous. The intention is for students to collect data and develop statistical skills through analysing the data and drawing conclusions.

Explore Mars Now

www.exploremarsnow.org

An interactive journey to Mars, where visitors can experience how life might be if they were to live on a space base built on the red planet.

ExploreLearning

www.explorelearning.com

ExploreLearning provides modular, interactive simulations in maths and science for teachers and students. Register as a member and you can enjoy the full benefit of this professionally designed site.

Extreme Science

www.extremescience.com

A handy resource for science homework detailing all the extremes in science – biggest, oldest, fastest, coldest, etc. The website also covers areas such as time, space, creatures, the weather and much more.

Fun Science

www.funsci.com

Fun Science has experiments for amateur scientists and students. This extensive site contains instructions showing how to put together low-cost scientific experiments. A useful resource for students and teachers.

Gemini Observatory

www.gemini.edu

An international partnership of two 8.1 metre telescopes, one situated in Hawaii and the other in Chile, thus covering both northern and southern skies. There are excellent resources here for astronomy enthusiasts.

Gondar Design Science

www.purchon.com

Designed by a British teacher, this site is popular with most of the educational directories and offers good material covering biology, chemistry, physics, ecology and health. The definitions database can be particularly useful while the virtual microscope section makes it all even more interesting.

How Stuff Works

www.howstuffworks.com

A brilliant website that lives up to its billing as the 'leading source for clear, reliable explanations of how everything around us actually works.' Technologies that we sometimes take for granted are explained here in plain language and with easy to understand charts and pictures.

Human Anatomy Online

www.innerbody.com

A fun, interactive site that is also an ideal reference for students. It is well animated with tons of graphics.

Implosion World

www.implosionworld.com

On the Implosion World website you can watch buildings being demolished and learn all about the science of demolition.

Institute of Physics

www.iop.org

The website of the leading international professional body and learned society which promotes the advancement and dissemination of physics.

Invention at Play

www.inventionatplay.org

Free your inventive mind through play. An extremely good interactive site that encourages you to 'explore the playful side of invention and the inventive side of play.'

MadSci Network

www.madsci.org

An edge-of-insanity site from the MadSci Network, a 'collective cranium of scientists' providing answers to scientific questions – some straightforward and some just weird. A fun site that asks some crazy questions, and gets some even crazier answers.

Mark Rothery's Biology Web Site

www.mrothery.co.uk

An experienced teacher and examiner, Mark Rothery built this site to help A level biology students. It contains extensive notes, summaries, past questions and other resources.

NASA – National Aeronautics and Space Administration

www.nasa.gov

This site has links to many space-related resources and there is a library of photographs, news stories and features. Science lesson plans and resources are featured in special sections for students and teachers.

Natural Hazards Education and Research Co-operative

www.naturalhazards.org

The NHERC is an educational, scientific and research organisation that aims to improve the understanding of natural hazards. Their attractive website is an extremely useful resource for students and teachers.

New Scientist

www.newscientist.com

The science journal that appeals even to non-scientists. The New Scientist has interesting, readable articles that simplify and explain often complex issues.

Noise – New Outlooks in Science and Engineering

Noise – New Outlooks in Science and Engineering

www.noisenet.ws

Bringing science alive by making it more accessible and relevant to young people. On this website you can have a look at the role that science plays in fashion, sport, music or entertainment.

Physics.org

www.physics.org

From the Institute of Physics comes this excellent interactive site with physics information to suit all ages and levels of knowledge. It matches your questions, age and knowledge to relevant resources that provide answers.

PhysicsWeb

www.physicsweb.org

The online version of Physics World magazine with news, features, analysis and links to some of the best physics sites on the web.

Planet Science

www.planet-science.com

This colourful and easy to navigate site is managed by NESTA, The National Endowment for Science Technology and the Arts. Their site aims to support creative, fun approaches to science learning and teaching and to inspire more young people to engage in science. It has great games, resources and ideas plus a special section for under 11s.

RedNova

www.rednova.com

The latest news, information and features about science, space and technology.

Royal Institution of Great Britain

www.rigb.org

The RIGB (or RI) aims to be 'the home for everyone interested in science, irrespective of whether they have a scientific background or not'. Since the RI was founded over 200 years ago, 14 of its resident scientists have received the Nobel Prize.

Royal Observatory Greenwich

www.rog.nmm.ac.uk

The Royal Observatory at Greenwich is a centre for all kinds of events, exhibitions, lectures and planetarium shows. Their website allows you on a great virtual tour.

Royal Society

www.royalsoc.ac.uk

The Royal Society is the UK's national scientific academy. Founded in 1660, it is dedicated to promoting excellence in science. It houses many useful resources and links for teachers of science.

Schoolscience

www.schoolscience.co.uk

Following the national curriculum for science, this site offers tailored help for scholars up to age 18 and is dedicated to showing how science at school relates to our world and everyday lives. There are sections for biology, physics and chemistry along with information for teachers and students.

Science Active

www.science-active.co.uk

A science resource designed to make chemistry easier to learn. The website is for secondary schools and colleges and has plenty of lesson materials and presentations.

Science, Art and Human Perception

www.exploratorium.edu

The museum of Science, Art and Human Perception is housed in San Francisco's Palace of Fine Arts. The Exploratorium is a collage of over 650 science, art, and human perception exhibits. It is a leader in the movement to promote museums as educational centres.

The Scientist

www.the-scientist.com

The online version of The Scientist magazine, reporting on and analysing current issues, events, research and discoveries in the field of life sciences.

Scirus

www.scirus.com

A comprehensive science-specific search engine.

Sodaplay

www.sodaplay.com

On Sodaplay's website you can design two-dimensional creatures and see them move. Once built, your creatures will bounce, giggle and roll. The virtual models can race against other creatures or can be displayed in a virtual zoo. This is an excellent way to play with physics knowledge and apply the laws of motion.

Space.com

www.space.com

A website that's bound to keep space fans entertained for hours. It is one of the best space sites on the net with lots for younger space explorers.

SpaceDaily

www.spacedaily.com

An online magazine from Australia with news and features about space issues.

SpaceWander

www.spacewander.com

Take a seat in the virtual space-shuttle cockpit and experience an exciting journey in space. All of the pictures on the website are real images from NASA.

Students for the Exploration and Development of Space

www.seds.org

SEDS is an independent, US student-based organisation that promotes the exploration and development of space by educating and enthusing young people.

Try Science

www.tryscience.org

Experience the excitement of contemporary science and technology through this attractive, colourful, interactive website aimed at young students and their teachers.

Volt Net

www.voltnet.com

It will come as a shock to learn that the ground beneath us is essentially one plate of a giant capacitor that is charged to about 500,000 volts. A high voltage site!

Web Elements

www.webelements.com

On Web Elements a periodic table, atomic orbitals, a chemistry dictionary and much more is available. It is a high quality source of information, for both professional scientists and students.

Windows to the Universe

www.windows.ucar.edu

An entertaining and user-friendly site with a wide range of material covering earth and space sciences. It is built on three educational levels to suit users of all ages.

Worldwide Web Journal of Biology

www.epress.com/w3jbio

This website features research in diverse disciplines of the biological sciences. Its interactive forums and contributions facilitate a dynamic ongoing dialogue between authors and readers.

Social Studies

A section of this category provides information on Religion, Sociology, Psychology and Citizenship as part of the National Curriculum. Broader topics such as the work of the Prince's Trust, statistics, the Police, the United Nations, national youth services and many more informative and useful links for students to explore are also included here.

21st Century Citizen

Adherents.com

A-Level Psychology

Association for the Teaching of the
    Social Sciences

BeliefNet

Bibles.Net

Black and Asian History Map

Britkid

Citizenship

Cool Planet

Coursework.Info

Do-it

Freud Museum

GCSE RE site

Geohive: Global Statistics

Interfaith

MENSA

Moving Here

National Statistics Online

Oxford School of Learning

People for the Ethical Treatment
    of Animals

Police

Population

Prince's Trust

Religion and Ethics

Social Science Information
    Gateway

Sociological Research Online

Sociology Central

Sociology Online

SocioSite

TheREsite

United Nations News

Voice of the Shuttle

Young People's Gateway

YouthNet UK

21st Century Citizen

http://21citizen.co.uk/live/citizenship

The 21st Century Citizen site, from the British Library, provides stimulating and contemporary online resources to support the new Citizenship curriculum for students aged 11–16 in the UK.

Adherents.com

www.adherents.com

Adherents provides detailed statistics and facts about more than 4,000 religions, charities, faith groups, tribes, cultures, etc from around the world.

A-Level Psychology

www.a-levelpsychology.co.uk

A Psychology Press website offering books and resources to students and teachers alike.

Association for the Teaching of the Social Sciences

www.atss.org.uk

The aim of the ATSS is to promote the teaching of the Social Sciences. Their website provides a wide range of resources of interest to teachers.

BeliefNet

www.beliefnet.com

A multi-faith e-magazine with inspirational, informative and thought provoking features and articles about religions from around the world and religious issues.

Bibles.Net

www.bibles.net

This website claims to be the internet's 'one directory of online bibles and biblical reference material'. You can read the bible online, search the bible, compare versions, undertake historical research and more.

Black and Asian History Map

www.blackhistorymap.com

From Channel 4, a gateway to websites about black and Asian history across the UK. The sites featured are split into time periods, subjects and regions.

Britkid

www.britkid.org

An interactive peek into the lives of a variety of British youngsters from different ethnic backgrounds. Learn from this website about different cultures and become aware of racial issues.

Citizenship

www.dfes.gov.uk/citizenship

From the Department for Education and Skills, this site provides a source of information about education for Citizenship in the curriculum for young people in schools and colleges in England. There are sections for teachers, pupils, parents and governors.

Cool Planet

www.oxfam.org.uk/coolplanet

Cool Planet is primarily intended for teachers in England, Scotland and Wales and their students. It aims to bring the global dimension to the classroom using the concept of Global Citizenship.

S 173

Coursework.Info

www.coursework.info

Coursework Information has a large UK-orientated academic database, including essays and coursework on a range of social science subjects.

Do-it

www.do-it.org.uk

The National database of volunteering opportunities in the UK. There are hundreds of opportunites and everything you need to know about voluntary work.

Freud Museum

www.freud.org.uk

A pioneer in psychoanalysis, Freud's theories are still used today. The museum offers a wealth of information and guidance.

GCSE RE site

www.gcsere.org.uk

A highly recommended site having all that is required to pass RE GCSE successfully. A clear and easy to understand content fills the coursework, revision and glossary pages. It also has a good search facility.

Geohive: Global Statistics

www.geohive.com

This website has information on economic statistics related to world population and organised by regions, countries, provinces and cities.

Interfaith

www.interfaith.co.uk

This site aims to bring together people from different faiths with an emphasis on religious tolerance.

MENSA

www.mensa.org.uk

The society welcomes people from every walk of life whose IQ is in the top two per cent of the population with the objective of enjoying each other's company and participating in a wide range of social and cultural activities.

Moving Here

www.movinghere.org.uk

200 years of migration to England is beautifuly illustrated in Moving Here's collection of digitised photographs, maps, objects, documents and audio items from local and national archives, museums and libraries.

National Statistics Online

www.statistics.gov.uk

The UK's official statistics website is a reflection of the country's population, economy and society at national and local level.

Oxford School of Learning

www.osl-ltd.co.uk

Primarily offering resources for teachers and students with an interest in business studies and economics, this site also has plenty to offer for sociology, psychology and religious studies. Real case studies, essay plans, online forums and a lot more are available on more than 700 pages.

People for the Ethical Treatment of Animals

www.peta.org

PETA believes that animals deserve the most basic rights and consideration of their own best interests regardless of whether they are useful to humans. The website has links to other animal abuse associations.

Police

www.police.uk

This website is all about how the UK police works with information on recruitment, related links and sections on crimes and appeals.

Population

www.population.com

A collection of news from around the world with a social impact. There is also a good collection of other web resources related to world population which is a plus.

Prince's Trust

www.princes-trust.org.uk

Through practical support including training, mentoring and financial assistance, The Prince's Trust helps 14–30 year olds realise their potential and transform their lives. It focuses its efforts on those who have struggled at school or been in care. Young people who have been in trouble and the long-term unemployed are also a priority. Investigate this thoroughly interesting site and see what it can offer you, you will be surprised what's out there!

Religion and Ethics

www.bbc.co.uk/religion

Objective and factual information about a wide range of religions. Easy to use and browse, the site includes interactive facilities like message boards, quizzes and e-cards.

Social Science Information Gateway

www.sosig.ac.uk

SOSIG provides a huge range of information online for students, researchers and practitioners in the social sciences.

Sociological Research Online

www.socresonline.org.uk

The articles and features in Sociological Research Online 'apply sociological analysis to a wide range of topics in order to demonstrate the value and relevance of sociology today'.

Sociology Central

www.sociology.org.uk

This website is a one-stop-shop for everyone interested in sociology. Teachers are encouraged to participate along with students interested in having their coursework reviewed.

Sociology Online

www.sociologyonline.co.uk

Sociology Online provides sociology news, relevant links and references to current political issues along with other resources specifically designed for the sociology student.

S 175

SocioSite

www2.fmg.uva.nl/sociosite

The University of Amsterdam offers this huge Social Science resource which is cleverly organised into subjects covering over 170 sociological subjects.

TheREsite

www.theresite.org.uk

The starting point for RE on the web, TheREsite provides extensive resources for students and teachers and links to further information. It includes special pages for infants, juniors and teenagers.

United Nations News

www.un.org/news

This website provides daily news reports from a United Nations' perspective.

Voice of the Shuttle

http://vos.ucsb.edu

Voice of the Shuttle is an ambitious project run by a professor in the English Department at the University of California where he is gathering specific content and resources to suit the study of the humanities.

Young People's Gateway

www.dfes.gov.uk/youngpeople

The Department for Education and Skills Young People's Gateway is the government's focal point for information and websites relating to young people. The new Gateway will direct people aged 11 to 19 to the subjects most useful to them such as exam help, careers choices and further and higher education options. There is one section for young people and a second for those working with young people.

YouthNet UK

www.youthnetuk.org

YouthNet UK, the country's first 'virtual charity' and one of the most groundbreaking national youth services, helping more than one million young people every month.

Special Needs

This category provides sites with information and resources on education, technology, health, societies, trusts, teaching resources, sports and recreational activities for all ages and abilities. A number of sites are run by those with special needs and offer support and advice for young people, their parents, guardians, carers and teachers. It would be useful to visit the other categories in this book, as many will also contain beneficial and enjoyable resources relating to this subject.

Ability Net

Abletogo

Afasic

After 16

American Sign Language

A-sites

Auditory Processing Disorder UK

A–Z to Deafblindness

BBC Ouch!

British Council of Disabled People

British Deaf Association

British Disabled Angling Association

British Dyslexia Association

British Sign Language

British Stammering Association

Capability Scotland

Council for Disabled Children

Disability

Disability Now

Disability Rights Commission

Disability View

DisabilityUK

Disabled Living Foundation

Dyspraxia Foundation

Family Fund

HE-Special

Hidden Impairments and Disabilities

Holiday Care

Invisible Disability Connections

Jobability

Lady Hoare Trust

LD Online

Listen Up

Lords Taverners

National Association for Special Educational Needs

National Autistic Society

National Bureau for Students with Disability

National Centre for Learning Disabilities

National Federation of ACCESS Centres

Royal Association for Disability and Rehabilitation

Scope

Signed Performances in Theatre

Simon's Raising Achievement

Special Education Resources on the Internet

Special Needs Family Fun

Special Olympics Great Britain

Special School

Speech Teach UK

Sport and Recreation for People with Disabilities

Teaching Resources And Information

TechDis

TinSnips

WebABLE

Whizz-Kidz

Yourable

S 178

Ability Net

www.abilitynet.org.uk

A website for people interested in getting advice related to making use of IT to help people with disabilities. Ability Net enables a wide range of services relating to the use of IT to be offered to people with all types of disabling conditions.

Abletogo

www.abletogo.com

An online guide to hotels, guest houses, self catering accommodation, caravans and holiday centres suitable for people with mobility difficulties.

Afasic

www.afasic.org.uk

Afasic is a parent-led organisation that helps children and young people with speech and language impairments and their families. It provides training and information for parents (and professionals) and produces a range of publications.

After 16

www.after16.org.uk

An impressive website for teenagers and young people in the UK who have an impairment or disability and who are looking at what opportunities and services may be available to them when they leave school.

American Sign Language

www.where.com/scott.net/asl/abc.html

A website dedicated to American sign language. It has a fingerspelling interactive dictionary which will show you how to fingerspell particular words and there are visual examples of the alphabet.

A-sites

www.nlb-online.info

From the National Library for the Blind, this website provides an online library portal of accessible websites for the visually impaired.

Auditory Processing Disorder UK

www.apduk.org

APDUK aims to promote greater understanding of auditory processing disorder in the UK, both amongst the general public and by educators and employers.

A–Z to Deafblindness

www.deafblind.com

For deafblind people and those interested in learning more. This site teaches the deafblind manual alphabet while there are extensive resources for both deafblind and deaf or blind people, and their helpers.

BBC Ouch!

www.bbc.co.uk/ouch

The BBC's website that reflects life as a disabled person. It is not a resource, but more about life, living, creativity, humour and a means to reflect experiences and thoughts.

British Council of Disabled People

www.bcodp.org.uk

The BCODP is run by disabled people to promote the full equality and participation of the disabled within UK society. They represent about 130 UK organisations run and controlled by disabled people.

British Deaf Association

www.signcommunity.org.uk

The BDA is the UK's national organisation run by deaf people for deaf people. Their mission is to build a strong and vibrant community of deaf people equipped with the skills and confidence to contribute to society as equal citizens.

British Disabled Angling Association

www.bdaa.co.uk

The British Disabled Angling Association is a registered charity that develops coarse, sea and game fishing opportunities for people with disabilities.

British Dyslexia Association

www.bda-dyslexia.org.uk

The BDA aims to influence government and other institutions to promote a dyslexia friendly society that enables dyslexic people to reach their potential.

British Sign Language

www.britishsignlanguage.com

This site uses moving pictures to show the basic signs for British sign language.

British Stammering Association

www.stammering.org

The website of the British Stammering Association. The national organisation providing information for, and support to, adults and children who stammer.

Capability Scotland

www.capability-scotland.org.uk

Scotland's leading organisation for the disabled, providing a range of services to support disabled people of all ages, and campaigning on their behalf.

Council for Disabled Children

www.ncb.org.uk/cdc

The Council for Disabled Children aims to raise awareness of the needs of children with disabilities, promotes their participation in decision making about their lives and contributes to the development of government policy and practice relating to disabled children.

Disability

www.disability.gov.uk

From the government's Disability Policy Division, this website provides policy information about disabled people's rights and information about UK disability legislation.

Disability Now

www.disabilitynow.org.uk

The online version of the campaigning newspaper Disability Now. This site has news, features, advice, adverts, links, an archive and a chat forum.

Disability Rights Commission

www.drc-gb.org

The Disability Rights Commission (DRC) is an independent body established by an Act of Parliament to eliminate discrimination against disabled people and promote equality of opportunity.

Disability View

www.disabilityview.co.uk

Inspired by Disability View magazine, this website aims to be a resource for anyone

looking for useful information on disability in the UK.

DisabilityUK

www.disabilityuk.com

An information and portal site operated by disabled people for everyone. It covers topics such as health, legal issues, charities, disabled products, carers and much more.

Disabled Living Foundation

www.dlf.org.uk

The DLF is the UK's leading disability charity providing advice and information on equipment and assistive technologies to enhance the independence of the disabled.

Dyspraxia Foundation

www.dyspraxiafoundation.org.uk

A UK charity that helps people to understand and cope with dyspraxia. A resource for parents, teenagers and adults who have the condition and for professionals who offer support.

Family Fund

www.familyfundtrust.org.uk

The Family Fund aims to ease the stress on UK families who care for severely disabled children under 16. They provide grants and information relating to their care, such as for holidays and leisure equipment.

HE-Special

www.he-special.org.uk

This is the web site of a group of families who home educate children with special educational needs.

S 180

Hidden Impairments and Disabilities

www.hi2u.org

A website supporting and creating awareness for people with hidden impairments which are sometimes known as invisible disabilities.

Holiday Care

www.holidaycare.org.uk

A UK holiday and travel information service for disabled people.

Invisible Disability Connections

www.dolfrog.com

A useful website for information on living with an invisible disability. This site provides links available on the internet for most of the invisible disabilities, particularly auditory processing disorder.

Jobability

www.jobability.com

The job site that helps disabled people to find work.

Lady Hoare Trust

www.ladyhoaretrust.org.uk

Lady Hoare Trust helps children with juvenile arthritis or severe limb disabilities by providing them and their families with practical and financial support.

LD Online

www.ldonline.org

This US site has much useful information about different learning difficulties for parents, teachers and other professionals.

Listen Up

www.listen-up.org

A well organised website providing information and products geared to the special needs of hearing impaired children and their families.

Lords Taverners

www.lordstaverners.org

The Lords Taverners have been raising money since 1950 'to give young people, particularly those with special needs, a sporting chance'.

National Association for Special Educational Needs

www.nasen.org.uk

NASEN is the leading UK organisation which aims to promote the education, training, advancement and development of those with special educational needs. There are useful resource and links to be found here.

National Autistic Society

www.nas.org.uk

The National Autistic Society champions the rights and interests of people with autism and ensures they and their families receive quality services appropriate to their needs.

National Bureau for Students with Disability

www.skill.org.uk

A national charity promoting opportunities for young people and adults with any kind of disability in post-16 education, training and employment.

National Centre for Learning Disabilities

www.ncld.org

The mission of the National Centre for Learning Disabilities (NCLD) is to increase opportunities for all individuals with learning disabilities to achieve their potential.

National Federation of ACCESS Centres

www.nfac.org.uk

A UK-wide network of specialist services that work together to facilitate access for disabled people to education, training, employment and personal development.

Royal Association for Disability and Rehabilitation

www.radar.org.uk

RADAR's mission is to promote change by empowering disabled people to achieve their rights and expectations by influencing the way that disabled people are viewed as members of society.

Scope

www.scope.org.uk

Scope is a disability organisation that supports people with cerebral palsy and their families. It campaigns on their behalf and provides information to the public.

Signed Performances in Theatre

www.spit.org.uk

SPIT is a national body that promotes BSL (British Sign Language) with interpreted performances of mainstream theatre. The organisation aims to ensure that deaf people have access to a broad range of theatre.

Simon's Raising Achievement

www.simonmidgley.co.uk

The work of a learning support teacher, this website provides helpful information and resources about the use of ICT for teachers and other professionals working with children whose first language is not English or those with specific learning difficulties.

Special Education Resources on the Internet

www.seriweb.com

A US site that has a collection of internet accessible information resources that are of interest to those involved in special education.

Special Needs Family Fun

www.specialneedsfamilyfun.com

This website offers family fun and disability resources to enhance the quality of family life for families with disabilities and special needs.

Special Olympics Great Britain

www.specialolympicsgb.org

SOGB's mission is to provide year round sports training and competition in a variety of Olympic-type sports for people with learning disabilities, of all ages and ability levels.

Special School

www.specialschool.org

A site that helps teachers, parents and professionals understand the workings of a special school for children with severe and profound learning difficulties.

Speech Teach UK

www.speechteach.co.uk

Speech Teach UK provide extensive resources to help parents, teachers and professionals support children that have speech difficulties.

Sport and Recreation for People with Disabilities

www.sportdevelopment.org.uk/ html/disabledaccess.html

A website covering disabled sports organisations, associations and agencies for those with an interest in sports and recreation for people with disabilities.

Teaching Resources And Information

www.schooltrain.info

An attractive website with teaching resources using simple text supported by pictures, plus information sources about deafness and language disorders.

TechDis

www.techdis.ac.uk

TechDis aims to improve provision for disabled staff and students in further, higher and specialist education through technnology. It provides advice and information resources via extensive web-based databases.

TinSnips

www.tinsnips.org

TinSnips provides tools for teachers of individuals with autistic spectrum disorders, related developmental disabilities and children with special needs.

WebABLE

www.webable.com

Disability-related internet resources. WebABLE's goal is to promote the development of technologies that ensure accessibility for people with disabilities to advanced information systems and technologies.

Whizz-Kidz

www.whizz-kidz.org.uk

Whizz-Kidz offers information, advice, support and practical help to provide disabled children with independent mobility and thus help them move from isolation to inclusion.

Yourable

www.youreable.com

A community-based website for disabled people that integrates information, products and services.

Sport and Activities

The world's most popular sports and activities are featured here together with details of clubs, associations and organisations dedicated to them. Whatever you want to do, from walking to fishing, from yachting to yoga, from football to netball, or even if you aspire to the Olympics, this category will take you to your area of interest. **For further leisure pursuits visit the Crafts and Hobbies section.**

2Pass	British Olympic Association
4thegame	Crash.Net
Amateur Rowing Association	cricket365
Auto-Cycle Union	Cycleweb
Autosport Magazine	Daily Sail
Badminton Association of England	England Hockey
BBC Sport	England Netball
BBC Sports Academy	English Institute of Sport
Beach Wizard	Equine World
BIKEmagic	Federation Internationale de Natation
Brit Ball	Fishing
British Cycling	Fishing4fun
British Fencing	Football Association
British Gymnastics	Girl Guides Association
British Judo Association	Golf Today
British Mountaineering Council	Highway Code

Horse and Hound Online

Ice Hockey League

International Association of Amateur
 Boxing

International Association of Athletics
 Federations

International Gymnast Magazine Online

International Rugby Board

International Ski Federation

International Tennis Federation

Lawn Tennis Association

Link Up Football

National Association of Karate and
 Martial Arts Schools

National Basketball Association

National Ice Skating Association

Olympic Movement

Planet Darts

Planet Rugby

Ramblers Association

Real Runner

Scout Association

Seconds Out

Sky Sports

Sport England

Sportzine

UK Athletics

UK Diving

UKClimbing

Walking Britain

Walter Lawrence Trophy

Wimbledon – The Championships

Women's Sports Foundation UK

World of Rugby League

World Squash Federation

Yachting World

Yoga Village UK

Youth Sport Trust

S 185

2Pass

www.2pass.co.uk

A great site for learner drivers and
bikers, with sound advice and mock
exams. It also has entertaining articles
and stories.

4thegame

www.4thegame.com

4thegame provides all the news, all the
reports, all the fixtures, all the teams,
managers, features and comments from
the Premiership.

Amateur Rowing Association

www.ara-rowing.org

The ARA's site has coaching tips
and advice as well as news, details of
events and lists of rowing clubs across
the UK.

Auto-Cycle Union

www.acu.org.uk

The website of the Autocycle Union, the
governing body of motorcycle sport in the
UK. It has news, events, reports and a
special section for young riders.

Autosport Magazine

www.autosport.com

The online version of the popular magazine covering all forms of auto racing with news, features, good links and a shop.

Badminton Association of England

www.baofe.co.uk

The BAofE promotes the development of the game from grass roots to local and county level through to the national squad.

BBC Sport

www.bbc.co.uk/sport

An impressive and comprehensive sports news site, updated minute-by-minute. It covers UK and world sports news.

BBC Sports Academy

www.bbc.co.uk/sportsacademy

A super BBC site that encourages youngsters to take up sport. It has information on basic skills, rules, contacts, chat and quizzes. Plus equipment advice and health guidance.

Beach Wizard

www.beachwizard.com

Created by surfing fans, this is a comprehensive guide to the best surfing beaches in Europe. There are lots of reviews and photo and surfers can add their own comments.

BIKEmagic

www.bikemagic.com

BIKEmagic has news, equipment reviews, advice, events and links which are all aimed at the UK's cycling community.

Brit Ball

www.britball.com

A complete online coverage of basketball in the UK and Ireland with reports, results and features.

British Cycling

www.bcf.uk.com

An information-packed website from the governing body for cycle sport in the UK covering BMX, cycle speedway, cyclo-cross, mountain bike, road and track.

British Fencing

www.britishfencing.com

This website has everything from the world of fencing in the UK. From how to start fencing and joining a local club to advice on equipment plus the latest news, results and rankings from around the world.

British Gymnastics

www.british-gymnastics.org

Comprehensive coverage of gymnastics in the UK from the website of the national sport's governing body.

British Judo Association

www.britishjudo.org.uk

News, events and features from judo across the UK, plus advice on how to get started in the sport from the British Judo Association.

British Mountaineering Council

www.thebmc.co.uk

A magazine site from the BMC which promotes the interests of climbers, hillwalkers and mountaineers.

British Olympic Association

www.olympics.org.uk

An informative site about the work of the BOA whose aim is to 'develop and protect the Olympic Movement in Great Britain in accordance with the Olympic Charter.'

Crash.Net

www.crash.net

A comprehensive site covering news about all forms of motor sports – whether four wheels or two – from around the world.

cricket365

www.cricketline.com

A comprehensive cricket site with news, results, features and analysis of the game from around the world.

Cycleweb

www.cycleweb.co.uk

The one-stop-shop for the everyday cyclist. On this website you can check out the latest cycling news, get information about events, buy and sell bikes, find out about local cycling clubs and much more.

Daily Sail

www.thedailysail.com

An online magazine with news and features from the world of sailing.

England Hockey

www.hockeyonline.co.uk

The website of the sport's governing body has more than just news and results. There is lots here about local clubs, coaching and how to get involved in hockey.

England Netball

www.england-netball.co.uk

The site to visit for everything about netball in England. It offers loads of advice on coaching, development and how to get involved in the game.

English Institute of Sport

www.eis2win.co.uk

The aim of the EIS is to support and foster the talents of the UK's best athletes. Their website is packed full of useful advice for any young sportsperson determined to make it to the top.

Equine World

www.equine-world.co.uk

Equine World provides comprehensive news and advice on horse-related issues from horse riding clubs to buying a pony.

Federation Internationale de Natation

www.fina.org

FINA is the world's governing body for swimming, diving, water polo, synchronised swimming and open water swimming.

Fishing

www.fishing.co.uk

Whether you're a beginner or a seasoned angler, this massive site has a mixture of news, features, tips and guides plus advice about the best places to fish and a message board where you can discuss the one that got away.

S 187

Fishing4fun

www.fishing4fun.co.uk

An online magazine-style site with oodles of information and tips for both beginners and professionals.

Football Association

www.thefa.com

The website of the game's governing body in England. It covers everything from the England national team to the women's game and grassroots football.

Girl Guides Association

www.girlguiding.org.uk

This UK site gives information on the Association and its activities. The World Association has four centres which welcome Girl Guides and Girl Scouts from all nations.

Golf Today

www.golftoday.co.uk

Probably one of the best onlife golf magazines. It has a huge array of golf news, features, rankings and tournament details.

Highway Code

www.highwaycode.gov.uk

The Highway Code online. This website contains essential road rules for pedestrians, drivers, cyclists and motorcyclists. If you are learning to drive or ride a motorcycle then this site is a must.

Horse and Hound Online

www.horseandhound.co.uk

News, reports, headlines and behind the scenes stories for equestrian enthusiasts. The website also provides advice on horse care, training, feed and veterinary issues.

Ice Hockey League

www.icehockeyleague.co.uk

This website keeps you up to speed with all that is happening in UK ice hockey. It includes news from the NHL and European leagues.

International Association of Amateur Boxing

www.aiba.net

The website of the world body for amateur boxing. It is a comprehensive site for serious boxing fans.

International Association of Athletics Federations

www.iaaf.org

An informative and detailed website from the governing body of world athletics. It includes details of the IAAF's work plus extensive news, results and lots more.

International Gymnast Magazine Online

www.intlgymnast.com

The online version of International Gymnast magazine with all the latest news, results, events and photos.

International Rugby Board

www.irb.com

A great site for world rugby from the International Rugby Board. The website contains results, fixtures, rules and advice on how to play and improve your game.

International Ski Federation

www.fis-ski.com

The official website of the International Ski Federation provides information on news, events and rankings and covers all forms of competitive skiing.

International Tennis Federation

www.itftennis.com

A jam-packed site from the tennis world's governing body, promoting and developing the game worldwide.

Lawn Tennis Association

www.lta.org.uk

This website contains not just news about the stars. It is dedicated to supporting tennis at all levels in the UK and includes tips and information about how to improve your game.

Link Up Football

www.linkupfootball.com

An extensive directory of football websites covering clubs, players, magazines, news, fanzines, kit and loads more.

National Association of Karate and Martial Arts Schools

www.nakmas.org.uk

NAKMAS is the governing body in the UK for all martial arts, traditional and modern. Their website is the best place to start for anyone interested in taking up the sport.

National Basketball Association

www.nba.com

The official site of the NBA, with all the statistics, features, analysis and chat that you could possibly need.

National Ice Skating Association

www.iceskating.org.uk

A comprehensive site from the sport's governing body, covering all forms of skating including dance, figure, speed and synchronised skating. The website offers advice on learning to skate and where to find your nearest rink and club.

Olympic Movement

www.olympic.org

The official website of the Olympic Movement. Discover the history of the Olympics, visit the museum and find out why the Olympic Games generates so much passion and enthusiasm amongst sportspeople around the world.

Planet Darts

www.planetdarts.co.uk

From the Professional Darts Corporation, this website has all the news, statistics, features, player profiles and tournament information from the world of darts.

Planet Rugby

www.planet-rugby.com

A comprehensive website presenting news, fixtures, results, rankings and player interviews from domestic and international rugby.

Ramblers Association

www.ramblers.org.uk

A wealth of information for beginners and experienced ramblers. The walks can be selected alphabetically, by region or by degree of difficulty.

Real Runner

www.realrunner.com

A well-designed and informative site for both runners and those who just follow the sport. The website provides health and equipment advice plus details of events, profiles and much more.

Scout Association

www.scouts.org.uk

The Scout Association helps young people to achieve 'their full physical, intellectual, social and spiritual potential' through providing enjoyable and attractive progressive training whilst guided by adult leadership.

Seconds Out

www.secondsout.com

An excellent site for boxing fans. It has news, results, analysis and opinion from boxing around the world.

Sky Sports

www.skysports.com/skysports

The Sky Sports news website gives extensive, regularly updated, coverage of a wide variety of sports.

Sport England

www.sportengland.org

The website of the government-backed organisation that creates opportunities for people to 'start in sport, stay in sport and succeed in sport'.

Sportzine

www.sportzine.co.uk

A directory of sports websites. Pick a sport, and Sportzine will suggest recommended sites and give you a comprehensive list of alternatives too.

UK Athletics

www.ukathletics.net

A lively site from the national governing body for athletics in the UK with news, features, details of events, clubs and guidance on how to get involved in the sport.

UK Diving

www.ukdiving.co.uk

On UK Diving you can find information about learning to dive, diving clubs, underwater photography and equipment plus a guide to wrecks. It claims to be the world's largest internet resource for divers.

UKClimbing

www.ukclimbing.com

An online magazine for serious climbing enthusiasts. It includes articles and features, UK and world climbing news, climbing forums, databases, photos and equipment reviews.

Walking Britain

www.walkingbritain.co.uk

A comprehensive and practical guide to walks around the UK. The walks are divided into region and graded. There are also features, links and photos plus advice on books, maps and walking gear.

Walter Lawrence Trophy

www.walterlawrencetrophy.com

Visit this site's hall of fame for background information on the winners of this prestigious Trophy, founded in 1934. The Trophy is awarded to the batsman who scores the fastest century in English first-class cricket each season.

Wimbledon – The Championships

www.wimbledon.org

This website includes anything and everything that is relevant about the Wimbledon tennis championships. It covers junior tennis as well as the star players.

Women's Sports Foundation UK

www.wsf.org.uk

The WSF aims to promote opportunities for women and girls to take part in sport and physical activity.

World of Rugby League

www.rleague.com

A comprehensive site with in-depth news, features and information about rugby league from around the world.

World Squash Federation

www.worldsquash.org

News, results, calendar, player rankings, rules, courts and much more about squash from around the world on this attractive site.

Yachting World

www.yachting-world.com

The online version of Yachting World magazine which includes all of the latest yachting news.

Yoga Village UK

www.yogauk.com

A comprehensive site about yoga in the UK. It also has lots of resources and links to other sites.

Youth Sport Trust

www.youthsporttrust.org

The YST's mission is to develop and implement quality PE and sports programmes for all young people in school and in the community.

Travel

This category has information to suit all ages, families, budgets and interests. Latest travel packages, tourism offices world-wide, maps, air ticket availability, holidays and guides can be found here. Search engines and travel information covering rail timetables, beaches, pet accommodation, hostels, student travel and trips for youngsters with teachers are also on offer here. **It may also be worth visiting Attractions, Museums, Careers and Students, and Sports and Activities.**

Association of British Travel Agents

Bananabuzz

Blue Flag

Brochurebank

BugBog

BUNAC

Continento

EcoClub

Ecovolunteers

Encounter Overland

Expedia

Family Fun – Travel

Fit For Travel

Fodors

Foreign and Commonwealth Office –
   Travel Advice

Frommers

Good Beach Guide

Great Outdoor Recreation Pages

Guardian Unlimited – Travel

Holidays Uncovered

Hostelling International

How to See the World

Insight Guides

i-uk

Knowhere Guide

Lastminute.com

LondonForFun

Lonely Planet

MapQuest

MultiMap

National Rail – Journey Planner

Neilson

Netcafeguide

Online Travel Plans

Pets On Holiday

Rough Guides

Seaside Awards

SeriousSports

STA Travel

Student Traveler

Time Out

Times Online Travel

Tips 4 Trips

Tour Britain

Tourism Offices Worldwide Directory

Towns Online

Transport for London

Travel Channel

Travel Intelligence

Travel Library

Travel Telegraph

TravelHealth

Travellerspoint

Travelmag

TravelNotes

UK Villages

Virtual Blackpool

Virtual Parks

VirtualTourist

Visit Britain

World Health Spa Directory

Youthtravel

Association of British Travel Agents

www.abtanet.com

ABTA is the UK's trade association for tour operators and travel agents. Their website has advice on travel related issues and is useful for researching specific destinations and for finding specialist travel companies.

Bananabuzz

www.bananabuzz.com

A virtual meeting place for backpackers from around the world. Members can update their profiles, interact with travelling buddies in the chat rooms or reunite with old travelling friends.

Blue Flag

www.blueflag.org

Find out from this website which beaches and marinas in Europe have Blue Flag status in recognition of their high environmental standards, water quality and safety.

Brochurebank

www.brochurebank.com

You can order free holiday brochures from this website. You just select your preferred destination and type of holiday.

BugBog

www.bugbog.com

A website offering independent and impartial travel advice to help you plan where to go and when. All of the best destinations, key information and tips. It is not so much a detailed reference work as an inspirational guide.

BUNAC

www.bunac.org.uk

A useful site from BUNAC, the independent national student club that organises work/travel programmes worldwide for students and young people. A must-visit site if you want to explore the world through a combination of work and travel.

Continento

www.continento.com

An interactive travel journal keeping track of your whereabouts wherever you may be in the world. Your friends and family at home can see your pictures and read your travel diary online.

EcoClub

www.ecoclub.com

Eco-travelling for people interested in protecting the environment while enjoying travelling. The site has ecotourism jobs worldwide, latest news, a student centre and a library plus relevant information from the experts.

Ecovolunteers

www.ecovolunteers.com

Ecovolunteers is a travel agency with a difference. They organise trips where you can help with conservation and other environmental protection projects. These are great working holidays for those with a keen interest in environmental issues.

Encounter Overland

www.encounter-overland.com

Encounter Overland provide adventurous active holidays and overland adventure travel in South America, Africa and Asia.

Expedia

www.expedia.co.uk

This is a veteran site from Microsoft packed with essential tools and trips for travellers including visa and passport information, airport guides and maps.

Family Fun – Travel

www.familyfun.go.com/family-travel

This website provides helpful information and advice for anyone planning a holiday with children and teenagers.

Fit for Travel

www.fitfortravel.nhs.uk

An extremely useful website from the NHS that provides travel health information for people travelling abroad from the UK.

Fodors

www.fodors.com

The famous travel guide, online. It has relevant, essential information well written and presented plus news, features and good links.

Foreign and Commonwealth Office – Travel Advice

www.fco.gov.uk/travel

The FCO's travel advice is designed to help British travellers to take informed decisions about their travel options. It has more than 200 country profiles plus advice on how to avoid trouble, especially threats to personal safety during political unrest, lawlessness, natural disasters, epidemics or demonstrations.

Frommers

www.frommers.com

An essential site to visit when planning travel abroad. You will find straightforward, no-nonsense travel writings and can read excerpts from Frommer's Guidebooks.

Good Beach Guide

www.goodbeachguide.co.uk

This website is from the Marine Conservation Society. The Good Beach Guide details the cleanest beaches in the UK in terms of water quality.

Great Outdoor Recreation Pages

www.gorp.com

An extensive website with masses of information about active travel world-wide and the outdoor lifestyle. It has inspiration for everything from an afternoon hike to biking holidays and the opportunity to share information through discussion groups.

Guardian Unlimited – Travel

http://travel.guardian.co.uk

The Guardian's super travel site has it all. Great reviews, interesting articles and features, travel news, budget travel, travelling with disabilities, eco tourism, gap year travel and more. The 'ask a traveller' section has an A to Z of tips and advice from fellow travellers.

Holidays Uncovered

www.holidaysuncovered.co.uk

Holidays Uncovered has over 20,000 reviews of holiday destinations and resorts written by genuine holiday-makers.

Hostelling International

www.hihostels.com

Hostelling International provides accommodation around the world for budget travellers, with 4,500 hostels in more than 60 countries. There are also links on this website to hostel websites.

How to See the World

www.artoftravel.com

An online travel book, entitled 'How to See the World', that gives clear and independent advice for budget travellers.

Insight Guides

www.insightguides.com

The website of the publishers of the world-famous travel guidebooks and maps. It has well written articles and oodles of essential information.

i-uk

www.i-uk.com/visiting

While aimed at visitors to the UK from abroad, i-uk is a great site for domestic tourists too. It covers all aspects of visiting the UK, from entertainment and leisure to useful tips for travellers, getting around and where to stay. An interesting feature archive and e-cards with images of Britain are also available and there are useful links to other websites.

Knowhere Guide

www.knowhere.co.uk

This website helps you to find the truth about places in the UK. Whether you are visiting or looking for fresh information about your home town, this site applauds the good and dishes the dirt on the bad for over 2,000 places throughout the UK.

Lastminute.com

www.lastminute.com

This website offers bargain travel and holiday deals. It also has entertainment, gifts and much more.

LondonForFun

www.londonforfun.com

An independent online guide to attractions and sightseeing in London.

Lonely Planet

www.lonelyplanet.com

Favoured by independent travellers, Lonely Planet has produced over 650 guidebooks covering every part of the world. Their extensive website is a great source of inspirational material.

MapQuest

www.mapquest.co.uk

A website providing detailed maps covering the whole of the UK. It can also give you driving directions; if you type in your starting point and where you want to go, MapQuest will give you directions.

MultiMap

www.multimap.com

A useful site for anyone travelling round the UK with material such as street level maps, road maps, door-to-door travel directions, traffic information and lots more.

National Rail – Journey Planner

www.nationalrail.co.uk/ planmyjourney

The online journey planner from National Rail.

Neilson

www.neilson.co.uk

Neilson have all sorts of active holidays including biking, sailing, surfing and much more.

Netcafeguide

www.world66.com/netcafeguide

A website helping you to keep in touch online while travelling. The Netcafeguide lists over 4,500 internet cafes around the world. If you enter the name of the city or town you are visiting, you will be given full details of internet cafes in your area, including opening hours and cost as well as location.

Online Travel Plans

www.onlinetravelplans.com

Keep your family and friends up to date when you are on your travels with this free email and storage service. This service 'was formed to provide the modern traveller with their every internet need'.

Pets On Holiday

www.pets-on-holiday.com

This website provides information on holiday accommodation in the UK that welcomes you AND your pets. It has extensive links to other websites.

Rough Guides

www.roughguides.com

From the producers of the superb Rough Guide travel books, this excellent website features online reviews of thousands of travel destinations. They also have music reviews covering every genre.

Seaside Awards

www.seasideawards.org.uk

The online guide to the cleanest beaches in the UK, with practical advice about how to get there and what to do when you arrive.

SeriousSports

www.serioussports.com

An extensive and easy-to-use directory site where you can find details of top-quality travel companies organising outdoor and adventure holidays.

STA Travel

www.statravel.com

The website of the agency that specialises in travel for students and young people.

Student Traveler

www.studenttraveler.com

Independent advice for student travellers from the online version of Student Traveler Magazine. This website includes information about working and studying abroad.

Time Out

www.timeout.com

Excellent guides to some of the most exciting and vibrant cities in the world taken from the Time Out Guide books.

The city guides provide information on accommodation, sightseeing, entertainment and special events.

Times Online Travel

www.travel.timesonline.co.uk

A brilliant, colourful, informative site from Times Newspapers that covers just about every aspect of travel. It is jam-packed with great articles, travel recommendations, practical advice and tips, destination reports, travel news and loads of inspirational features.

Tips 4 Trips

www.tips4trips.com

Tips 4 Trips contains thousands of practical travel tips submitted by travellers. It covers a range of topics such as safety, travelling with children, pets, books and packing.

Tour Britain

www.tour-britain.com

An online booking service and travel information guide covering the UK and Ireland.

Tourism Offices Worldwide Directory

www.towd.com

The title says it all. A directory of official tourism information services from around the world. It is excellent for research before you travel.

T197

Towns Online

www.towns-online.co.uk

A neat site that provides local and historical information about towns and cities across the UK.

Transport for London

www.cclondon.com

London's transport secrets are now online. This website has loads of information from the history of London's buses to weather or transport fares. The good reasons behind the congestion charges are also part of the rich content of this site.

Travel Channel

www.travelchannel.co.uk

The travel Channel brings entertaining and inspiring travel programming together with impartial holiday advice from around the world.

Travel Intelligence

www.travelintelligence.net

A well-designed site with some of the best travel articles on the internet, all written by well-informed travellers.

Travel Library

www.travel-library.com

Firstly, this website is a library of travelogues and other travel writing. Secondly, it has information and advice to help you plan your trip, such as transportation methods, money matters, visas, health issues and local customs. All you have to do is pick your destination!

Travel Telegraph

www.travel.telegraph.co.uk

This website has simply great travel writing from some of the best writers in the business.

TravelHealth

www.travelhealth.co.uk

A very comprehensive site with travel health advice, articles, books, links and more.

Travellerspoint

www.travellerspoint.com

An online travellers community where you will find tips and advice from fellow travellers and locals. You can share your travel experiences with friends and submit your own travel tips.

Travelmag

www.travelmag.co.uk

Travelmag has some of the finest travel writing in the world. Some of the articles and features are written by experienced journalists and travel writers, others by ordinary tourists who just have something interesting to write about.

TravelNotes

www.travelnotes.org

A comprehensive online travel guide that provides essential and extensive travel information including country background notes. There are also reviewed websites plus travel features and articles.

T 198

UK Villages

www.ukvillages.co.uk

Community-focussed information links for every village in the UK.

Virtual Blackpool

www.blackpool.com

This website provides a virtual tour of the UK seaside resort. Blackpool is the traditional British seaside holiday.

Virtual Parks

www.virtualparks.org

On this website you can pay a virtual visit to some of the world's greatest wilderness areas through panoramic photography. There are 360 degree photos of stunning scenery.

VirtualTourist

www.virtualtourist.com

Described as 'the world's leading online travel research exchange', VirtualTourist has over 400,000 members from 220 countries and territories who share their travel experiences and insights in order to help others 'travel smarter.'

Visit Britain

www.visitbritain.com

The excellent official website for visitors to the UK, from Visit Britain. It is great for domestic tourists too. A treasure trove of tourism information and advice.

World Health Spa Directory

www.worldhealthspa.com

A directory site that provides an extensive selection of spas and other health resorts around the world. You can search by location and the type of treatment offered.

Youthtravel

www.youthtravel.com

The website of the 'wallet friendly' travel service that specialises in discount travel for students and other young travellers.

Younger Children

This section is mainly for children aged 5 to 13. It covers National Curriculum subjects studied in primary schools and contains sites that are educational, entertaining and stimulating. There are interactive games and activities to encourage youngsters to play and learn, as well as special interest subjects such as pets, music, space, archaeology, and much more. **Additional suitable websites for this age group are available in many of the individual categories, although it is important to remember that parents may need to offer guidance and support for smaller children when using the internet.**

Achuka Children's Books

Animals

Art Attack

Ask Jeeves – Kids

At School

BBC ReviseWise

BBC Schools – Ages 4–11

BBC Schools – Megamaths

BBC Schools – Words and Pictures

BBC Science and Nature: Animals

Blue Peter

Bug Club

Bullying Online

Cat Protection League

CBBC Newsround

ChildLine

Children's Music Web

Creating Music

Dance Kids

Discovery Channel

Dragonfly

Enchanted Learning

Eureka!

Galaxy-H

Global Warming

Goosebumps

Grid Club

Harry Potter

Hedgehogs

Inventive Kids

Juniors

Kaboose

Kennel Club

Kids' Space

KidsOp

National Geographic – Kids

Pet Website

PetPlanet

Planet Science

Play Music

Puffin

Rabbit Welfare Association

Schoolfriend

ScienceWeb

Scribbles Kids Art Site

Show Me

Sunshine Online's Literacy Hour

Teaching Tables

Television Heaven – Kids' Corner

Udside

UK Safari

Welltown

Young Archaeologists Club

Young TransNet

Youth Music – The Sound Station

Yucky.com

Achuka Children's Books

www.achuka.co.uk

An independent children's book site where you can keep in touch with the latest books, find out more about your favourite authors and share your views about books.

Animals

www.seaworld.org

Helping you to explore, discover and connect with animals. This website aims to bring the excitement, wonder and awe of the natural world into homes and schools. It is a good resource for teachers and parents.

Art Attack

www.hitentertainment.com/ artattack

The Art Attack website has fact sheets showing hundreds of arty and creative things to do and make plus lots of inspirational ideas to keep you busy and creative.

Ask Jeeves – Kids

www.ajkids.com

A safe search engine for children that is good for homework questions and games too.

At School

www.atschool.co.uk

The atschool website has been developed with both inexperienced and frequent internet users in mind. atschool will help parents and teachers to help children use the internet for education at school or in the home.

BBC ReviseWise

www.bbc.co.uk/revisewise

A helpful site for 10–11 year olds preparing for Key Stage 2 national curriculum tests in English, maths and science.

BBC Schools – Ages 4–11

www.bbc.co.uk/schools/4_11

Part of the excellent BBC Schools website, this area is aimed at children aged 4 to 11. It includes learning resources for home and school covering all curriculum subjects.

BBC Schools – Megamaths

www.bbc.co.uk/education/ megamaths

This interactive site provides lots of fun for primary school children as they learn about multiplication tables and shapes.

BBC Schools – Words and Pictures

www.bbc.co.uk/education/ wordsandpictures

This BBC site, targeted at 5–7 year olds, is full of inspirational and entertaining games and activities to help children develop their knowledge of phonics. It is excellent for children both at school and at home.

BBC Science and Nature: Animals

www.bbc.co.uk/nature/animals

A very attractive site with inspirational content about animals and the natural world. It includes a section on pets and a children's zone.

Blue Peter

www.bbc.co.uk/cbbc/bluepeter

The website of the well-known, long-running children's television programme is colourful and packed with information, games and competitions.

Bug Club

www.ex.ac.uk/bugclub

Insects make up about 80 per cent of all known species and The Bug Club is dedicated to young people who find insects and other bugs and creepy crawlies interesting and fascinating. It even includes advice on how to keep bugs as pets.

Bullying Online

www.bullying.co.uk

This site is very helpful for learning what to do about being bullied at school. It has good advice too for parents and teachers about how to deal with the problem.

Cat Protection League

www.cats.org.uk

The UK's oldest and largest feline welfare charity, Cats Protection rescues and rehomes unwanted and abandoned cats. It also advises how to look after your cat responsibly.

CBBC Newsround

www.bbc.co.uk/cbbcnews

The BBC's superb children's news site makes UK and world news interesting and engaging for young people.

ChildLine

www.childline.org.uk

The 24 hour helpline for children in distress or danger. The site doesn't provide advice online, but it is a great place for children to find information on issues of concern to them. It has other helpful links too and details on how to contact them if you have a problem or want someone to talk to.

Children's Music Web

www.childrensmusic.org

Children's Music Web provides online music resources for kids, children's performers, teachers and parents worldwide.

Creating Music

www.creatingmusic.com

A website that provides children of all ages with an environment to experience creative play in the creation of music. It's a place where they can compose music, play music games and solve music puzzles.

Dance Kids

www.dance-kids.org

The interactive website for youngsters who love to dance, with games, quizzes, stories, gallery and more.

Discovery Channel

www.discovery.com

An excellent website from the television channel. It has a huge range of topics, plus live webcams. There's lots here to keep children interested.

Dragonfly

www.muohio.edu/dragonfly

Dragonfly aims to involve children in the creative process of science in order to help them see how science relates to their lives. Dragonfly's website is full of everyday events and questions such as what happens when you flush the toilet and what is pollution?

Enchanted Learning

www.enchantedlearning.com

This huge US site is ideal for rainy days. It has plenty of interesting information, features and activities to choose from plus hobbies, quizzes, crafts, educational resources and more.

Eureka!

www.eureka.org.uk

What happens to the food we eat? How are television programmes made? This site has the answer to these and other questions about everyday life and the world in which we live.

Galaxy-H

www.galaxy-h.gov.uk

Visit the Galaxy-H space station to find out about keeping healthy and staying safe. Galaxy-H is aimed at 7–11 year olds and covers the main areas of personal, social and health education and citizenship as set out in the national curriculum.

Global Warming

www.epa.gov/globalwarming/ kids

A lively and informative site from the US Environmental Agency which explains the basis of global warming and the greenhouse effect using animation and games plus information on how you can make a difference.

Goosebumps

www.scholastic.com/goosebumps

Spooky online interactive fun and games from Goosebumps, the writers of scary books for children. On the website you can play scary fun and games, send cards to your friends, play some ghostly games and check out the latest Goosebumps books.

Grid Club

www.gridclub.com

An interactive learning site for 7 to 11 year olds. The website includes Thesaurus, dictionary, facts, figures and activities covering science, history and geography plus help with homework and projects which are all presented in a colourful and fun way.

Harry Potter

www.harrypotter.warnerbros. co.uk

The official Harry Potter website from the makers of the films. A well-designed, top quality site with reviews and information, games and music from all the Harry Potter movies.

Hedgehogs

www.hedgehogs.gov.uk

The Hedgehogs website is packed full of games and sing-along songs to help children learn about road safety.

Inventive Kids

www.inventivekids.com

An interactive Canadian site that provides an easy to use, fun and effective teaching tool on invention and innovation. It is useful both at school and at home, with a wealth of valuable information for school students.

Juniors

www.juniors.net

Action-packed fun learning online for 7 to 11 year olds, with over 850 exciting,

interactive activities to choose from covering literacy, numeracy and science.

Kaboose

www.kaboose.com

Kaboose's 'Funschool' pages offer over 800 interactive games and activities for children up to age 11 that are fun, easy to use and educational.

Kennel Club

www.the-kennel-club.org.uk

The Kennel Club promotes responsible dog ownership. Their attractive website is jam-packed with information and advice for dog owners, covering topics such as health, insurance, training and feeding. They have a Young Kennel Club for young dog lovers. The Kennel Club also organises the famous Crufts dog show.

Kids' Space

www.kids-space.org

This US site is designed to be a sharing space where children worldwide can explore and communicate. Amongst the many sections you will find illustrated stories by children from around the world, pictures where children can provide the words and a concert hall where sound files of childrens' own musical performances can be put online.

KidsOp

www.kidsop.com

A Canadian opera company that creates new operas for children (8–15) and adults to perform together, and facilitates the production of the operas internationally. You can see the joy of children discovering and performing opera, the wonder of opera that the children bring to the adults working with them and the magic of opera brought to the audiences who see the performances.

National Geographic – Kids

www.nationalgeographic.com/kids

National Geographic's attractive site for young readers contains vast information about the world, its people and its wildlife. There are useful encyclopedia links, great games, interactive activities, stories and features too.

Pet Website

www.petwebsite.com

A great website with extensive information about hamsters, dogs, cats, gerbils, mice and many more pets. There is an in-depth guide to the various species, health and care advice, plus links to breeders, clubs and shows.

PetPlanet

www.petplanet.co.uk

PetPlanet claims to be the UK's leading website about dogs, cats and other pets. The website contains information and articles plus pet products.

Planet Science

www.planet-science.com

This colourful and easy to navigate site is managed by NESTA, The National Endowment for Science Technology and the Arts. The site aims to support creative, fun approaches to science learning and teaching and to inspire more young people to engage in science. The website includes great games, resources and ideas, plus a special section for the under 11s.

Play Music

www.playmusic.org

For younger children, this website is a valuable tool in describing instruments and hearing what sounds they make.

Puffin

www.puffin.co.uk

The Puffin website has lots of fun and free stuff plus parents' and education zones. There is also detailed information about Puffin children's books with a database of the full range of titles and recommendations for different age groups.

Rabbit Welfare Association

www.rabbitwelfare.co.uk

The Rabbit Welfare Association dedicates itself to helping you look after your rabbit's welfare.

Schoolfriend

www.schoolfriend.com

Interactive web-based learning courses for 4 to 13 year olds, concentrating on maths, spelling and vocabulary. It is suitable for school or home. The prime content is available to subscribers only but the free content can give you an idea about the value of the courses on offer.

ScienceWeb

www.scienceweb.org.uk

ScienceWeb offers ready-made, easy to use, fun worksheets and interactives to support the teaching of science to primary school children.

Scribbles Kids Art Site

www.scribbleskidsart.com

For young artists and art teachers with lots of topics, tasks and colours to choose from to help develop childrens' artistic natures. This US site not only encourages children to be creative but also informs them about different artists and their work.

Show Me

www.show.me.uk

Show Me is the children's section of the 24 hour Museum website. The site is packed with online games, resources and interactive content produced by the UK's museums and galleries.

Sunshine Online's Literacy Hour

www.literacyhour.co.uk

Lesson plans, shared reading, web and learning activities are just a few of the resources available here. This is a complete resource to support teachers in developing literacy skills at Key Stages 1 and 2.

Teaching Tables

www.teachingtables.co.uk

Teaching Tables is a resource for teachers. It is a fun way for the class to practice their multiplication.

Television Heaven – Kids' Corner

www.televisionheaven.co.uk/kids.htm

The Kids' Corner section of the Television Heaven website is devoted to preserving the memory of classic children's cartoon and puppet shows, past and present.

Udside

www.udside.co.uk

A fun and innovative site that complements work on the personal, social and health education and citizenship areas of the national curriculum, specifically drug education. The site is aimed at pupils aged 9–11 and is designed to be used by children in schools either as individuals or in groups.

UK Safari

www.uksafari.com

An attractive and informative site that will be of interest to anyone interested in the British countryside. The site provides information about the amazing flora and fauna that can be found in and around the UK.

Welltown

www.welltown.gov.uk

Welltown is aimed at Key Stage 1 pupils, aged 5–7 years, and covers the main areas of personal, social and health education and citizenship set out in the national curriculum. It can be used at school or at home, by children on their own or in groups.

Young Archaeologists Club

www.britarch.ac.uk/yac

If you are interested in archaeology then you should consider joining the YAC which is open to young people aged 8 to 16. You can take part in a residential holiday, enter the Young Archaeologist of the Year Award and find out about the latest discoveries.

Young TransNet

www.youngtransnet.org.uk

Young TransNet aims to increase walking, cycling and the use of public transport, and to reduce motor traffic. It uses IT and the internet to assist children and young people in transport research and action.

Youth Music – The Sound Station

www.thesoundstation.org.uk

Enabling young people to make themselves heard musically – regardless of age, background or ability – Youth Music funds music-making projects across the country. Visit this site to see what Youth Music is doing in your area.

Yucky.com

www.yucky.com

An excellent site that educates and amuses children in the wonderful world of 'yucky' science. It is certain to keep kids captivated for hours.